INSPIRIT MANDALAS

By Lirio M. Jiménez

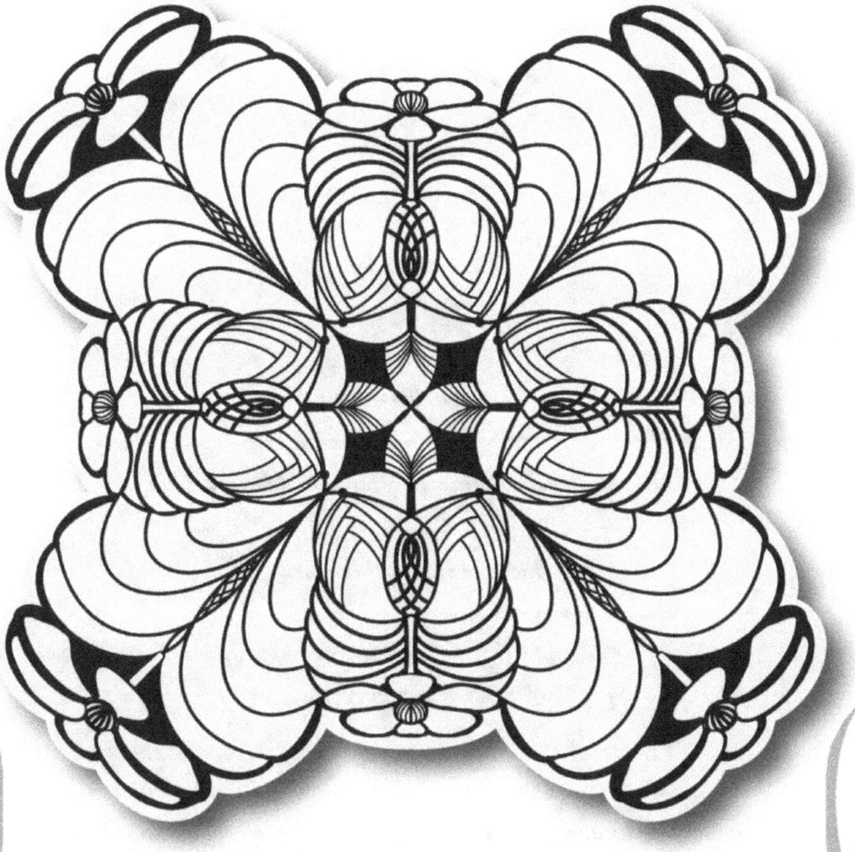

Published by

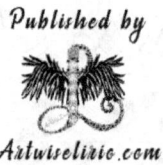

Artwiselirio.com

Lirio M. Jiménez, Inspirit Mandala Coloring Book
1st published 2023 USA
Independantly Published

This adult coloring book is meant to refresh your spirit from the overwhelming day to day, that is life. Helping you find a connection to peace and serenity that there is when engulf in coloring.

Inside are 60 mandalas for your enjoyment.

Inspired in:

·Fruits, Flowers and Leaves.

· Animals, Insects and Sea Life.

·Pinwheels and Abstracts

Let your spirit be healed with the restorative effects of Art. Be caring to you, by taking the time to allow your spirit room to play.

Allowing your spirit to heal.

Go ahead try it!

Art 2 heal Art 2 chill

All ages 13 and up.

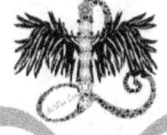

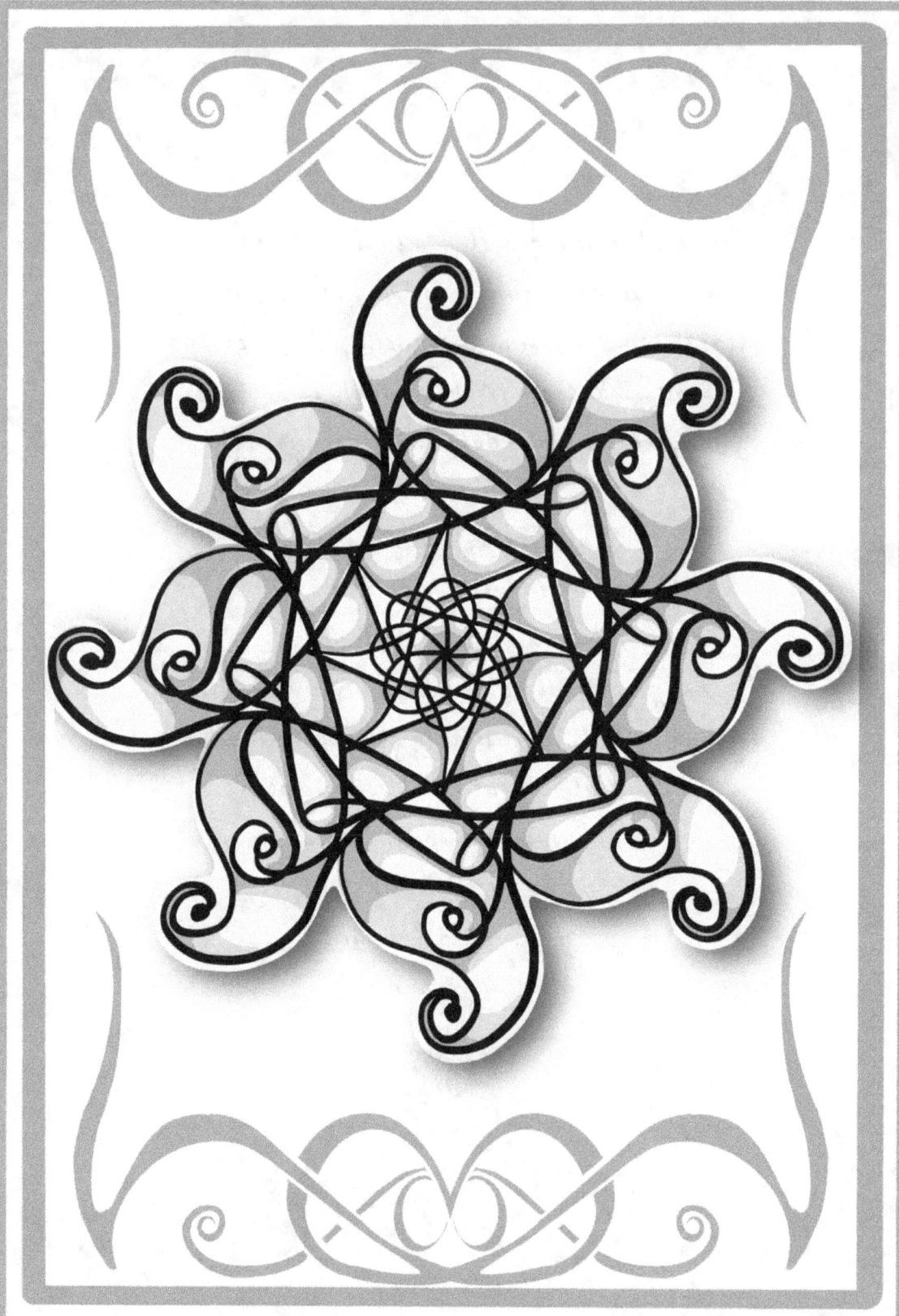

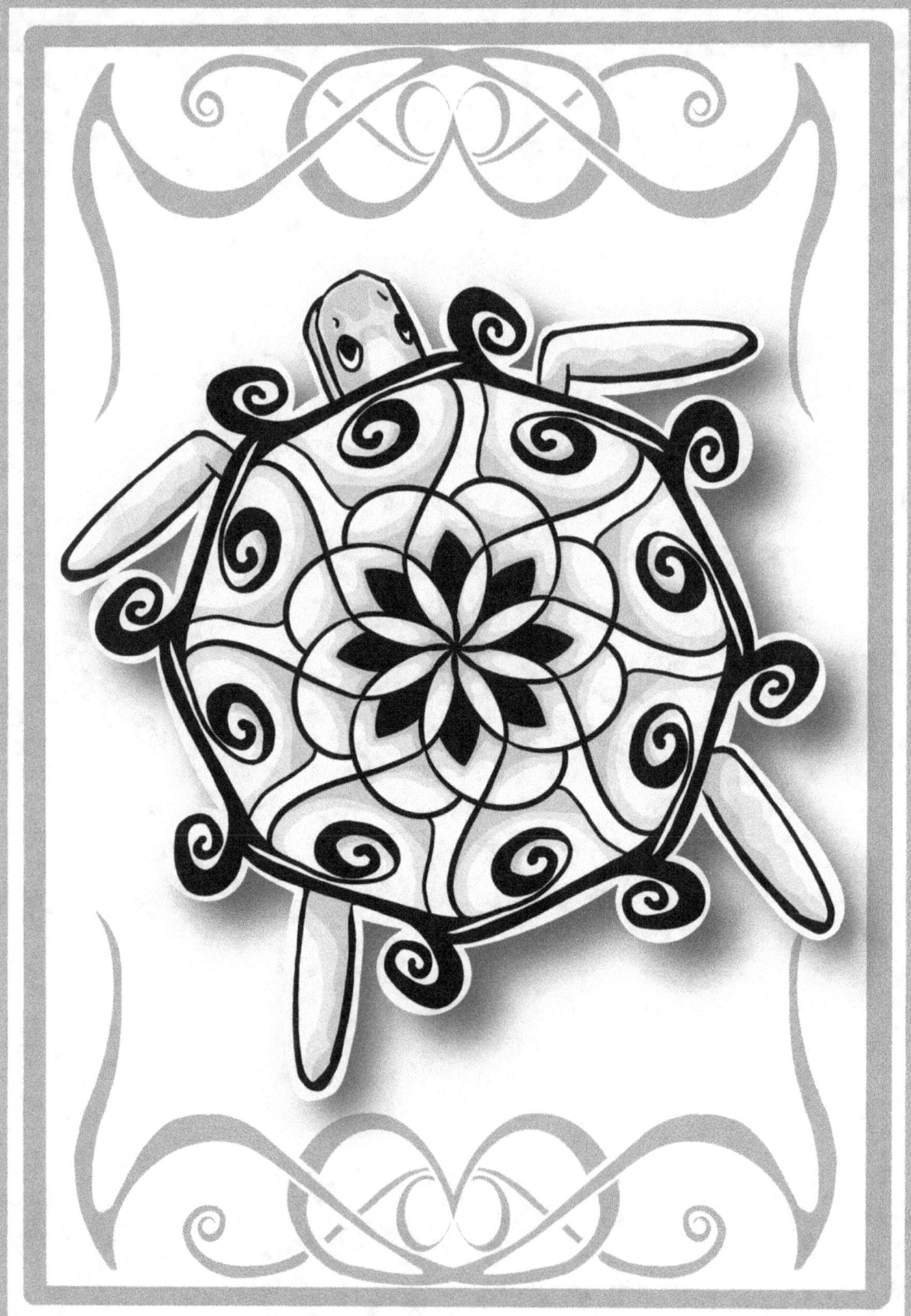

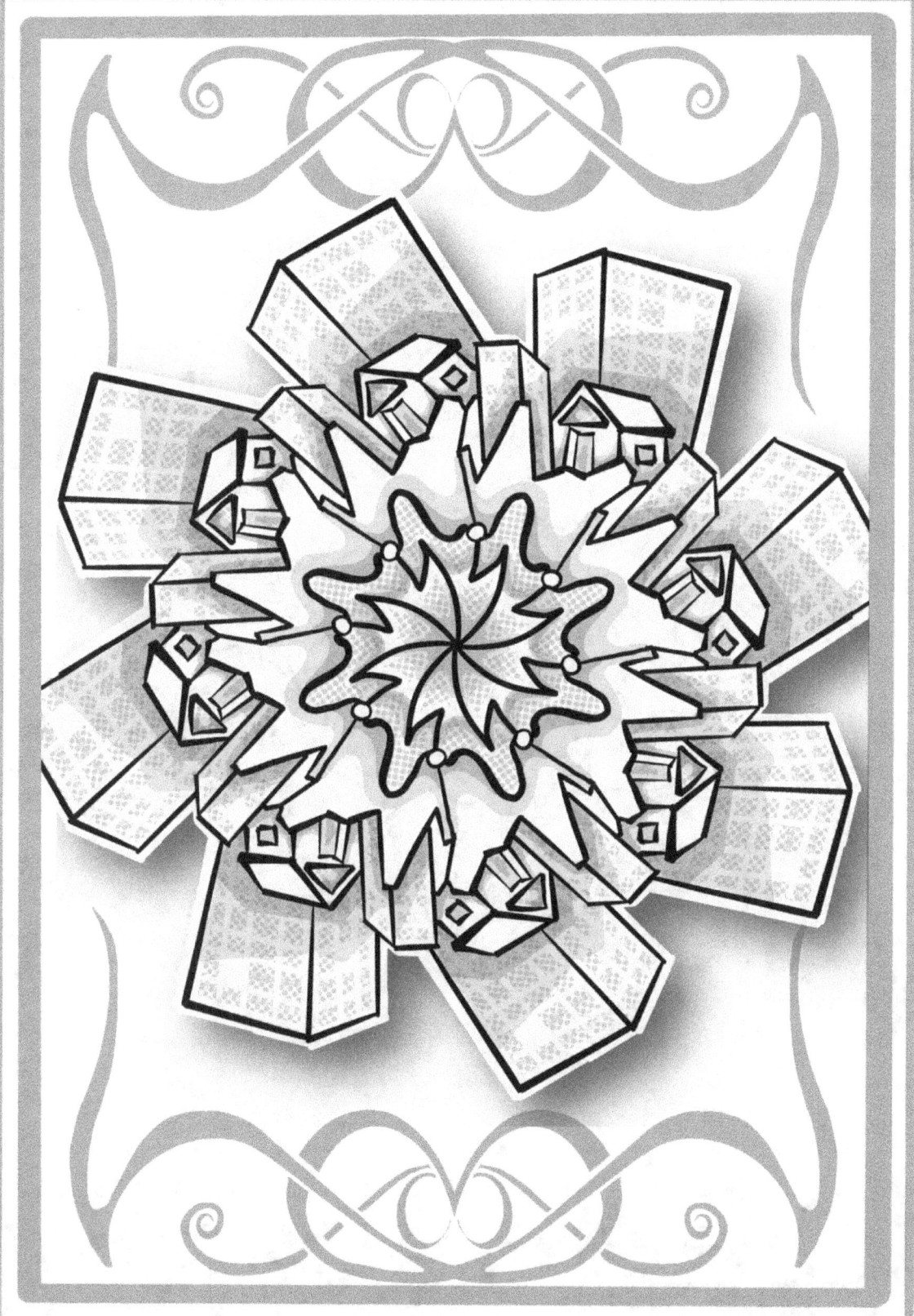

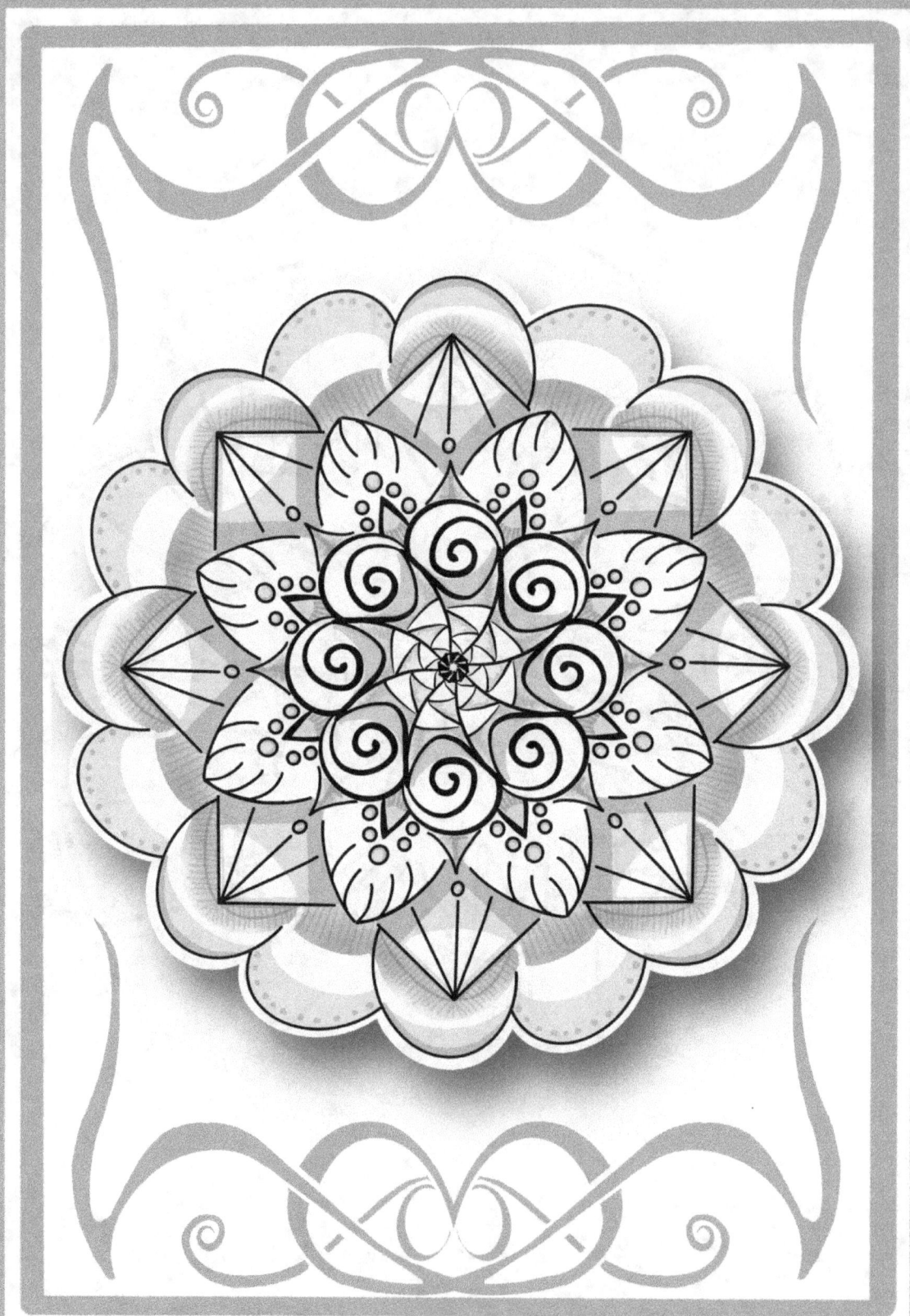

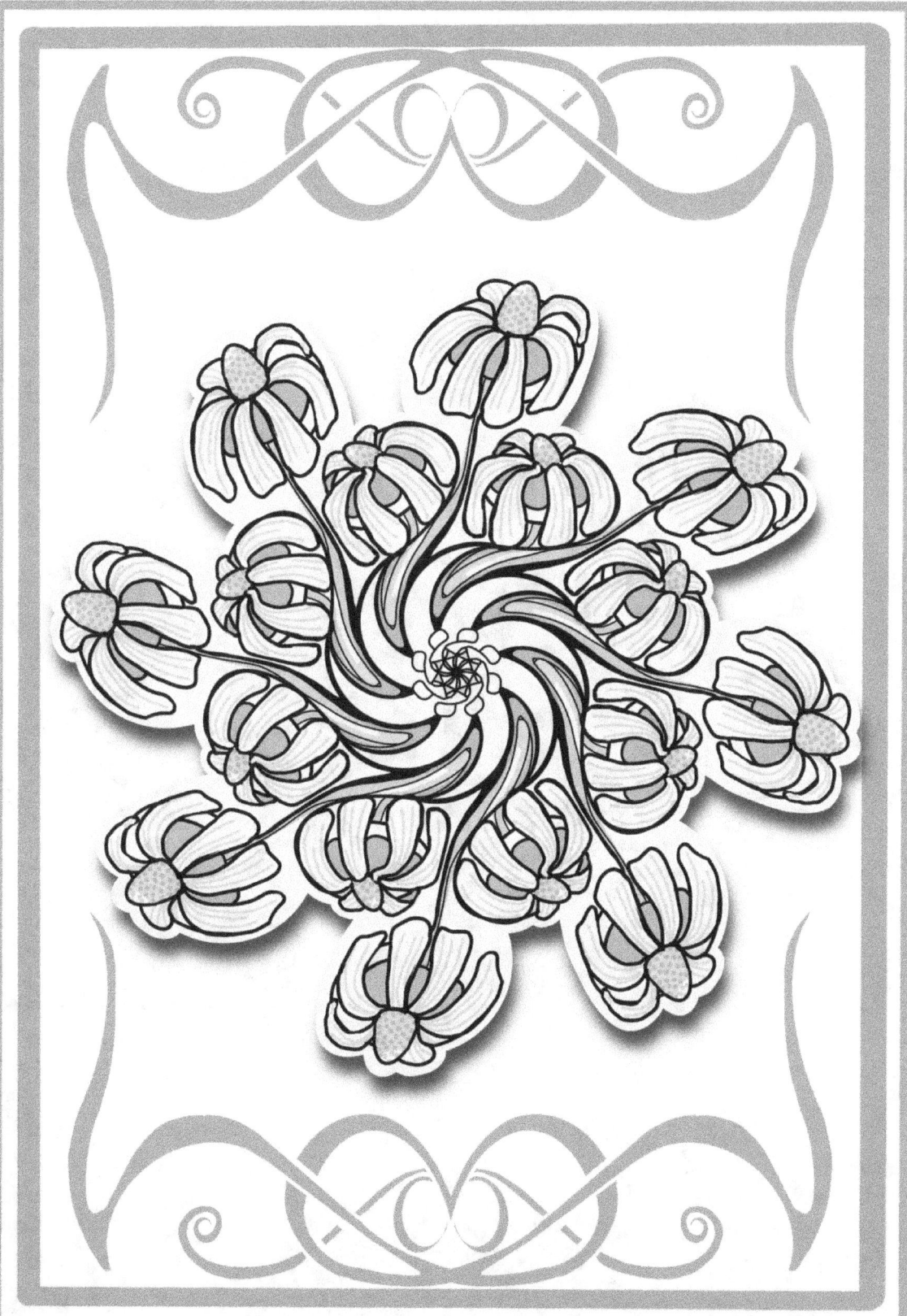

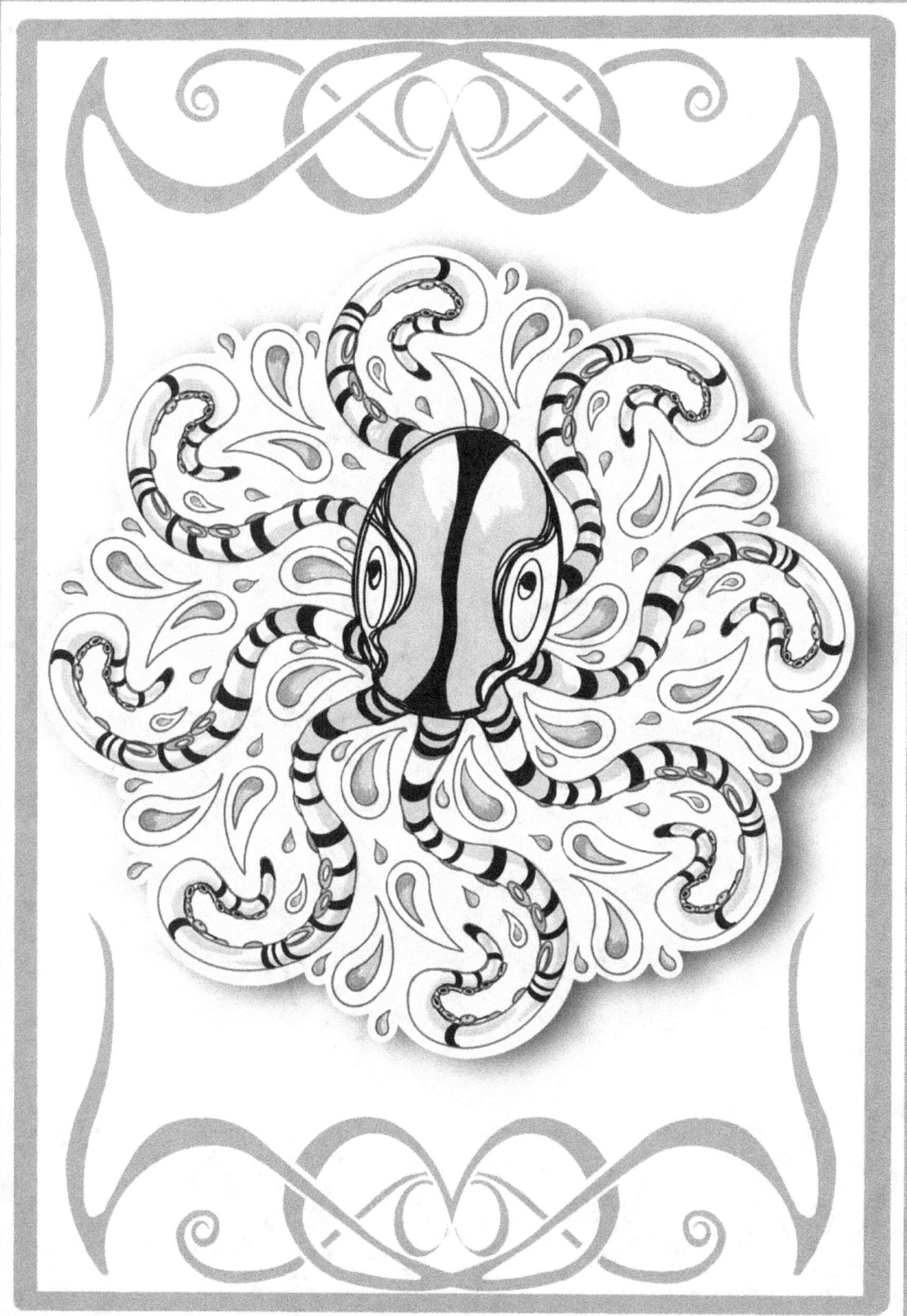

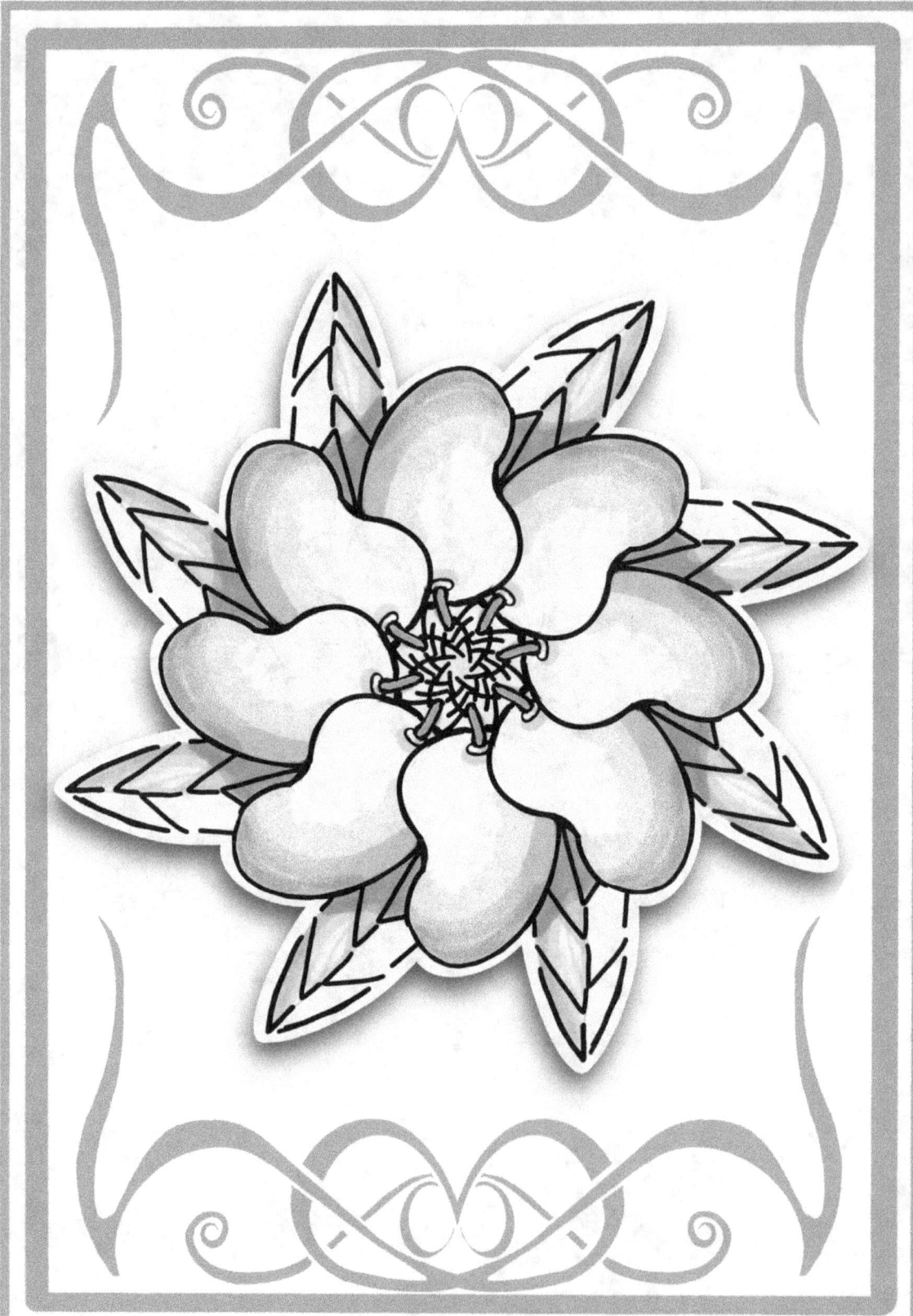

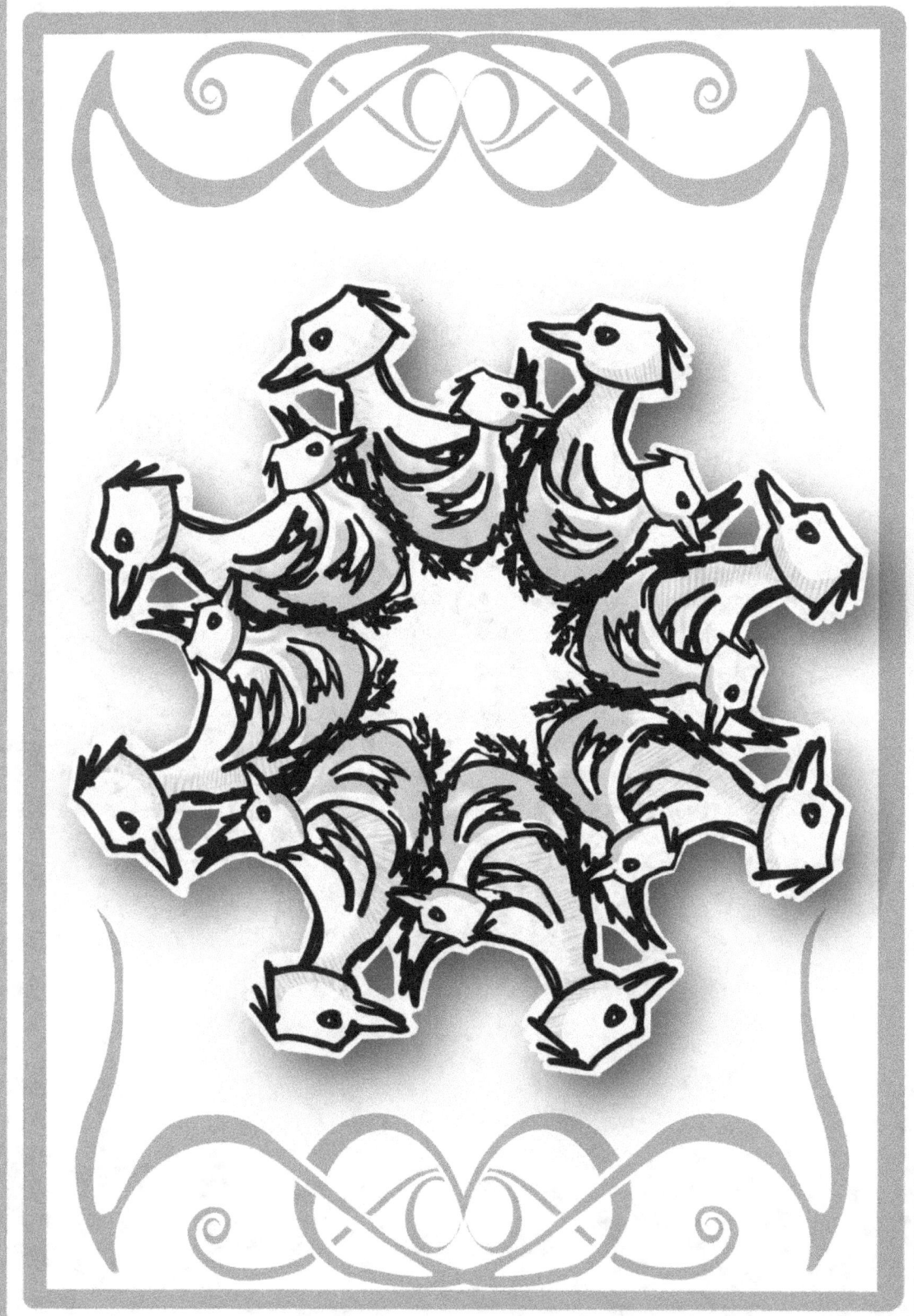

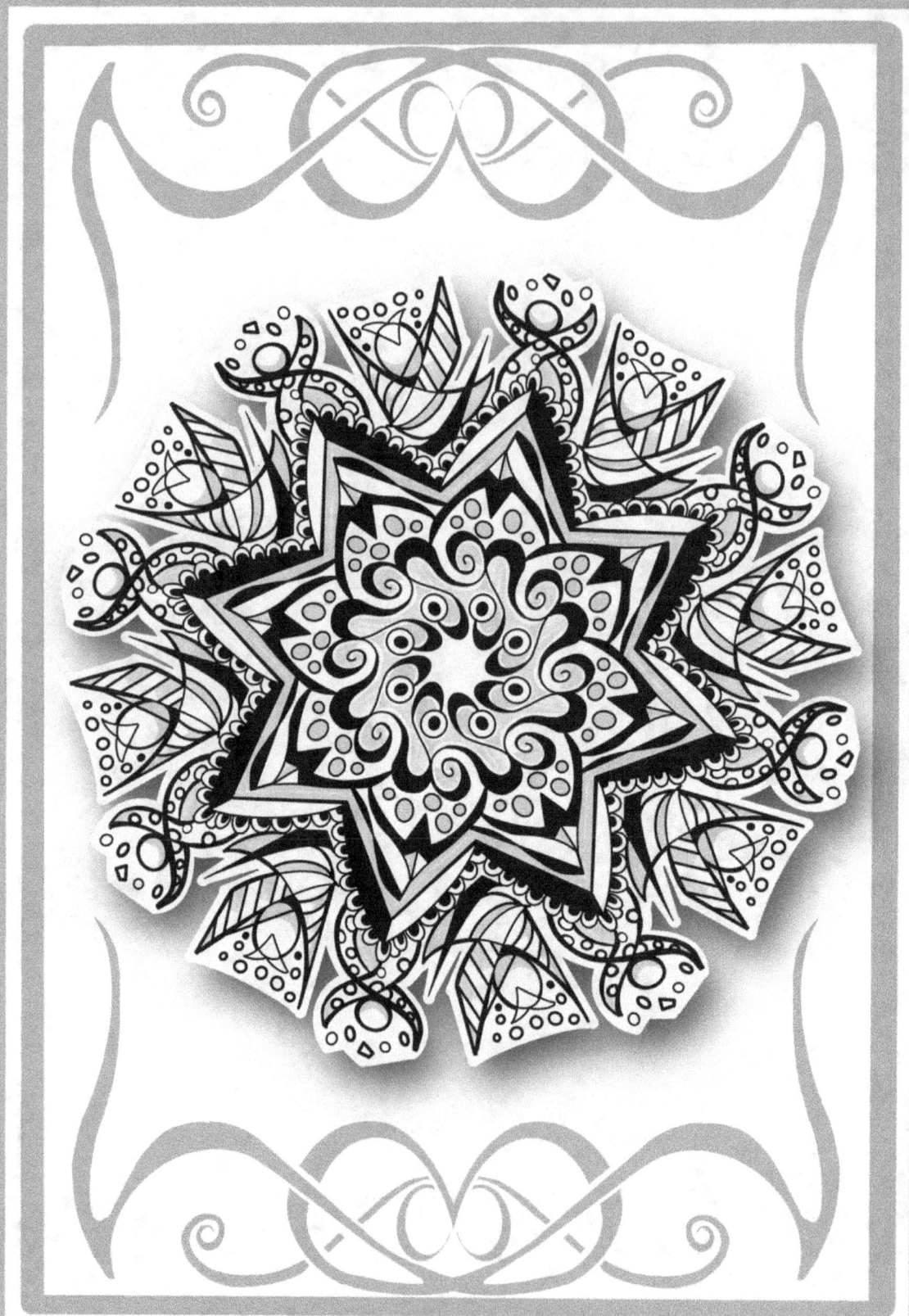

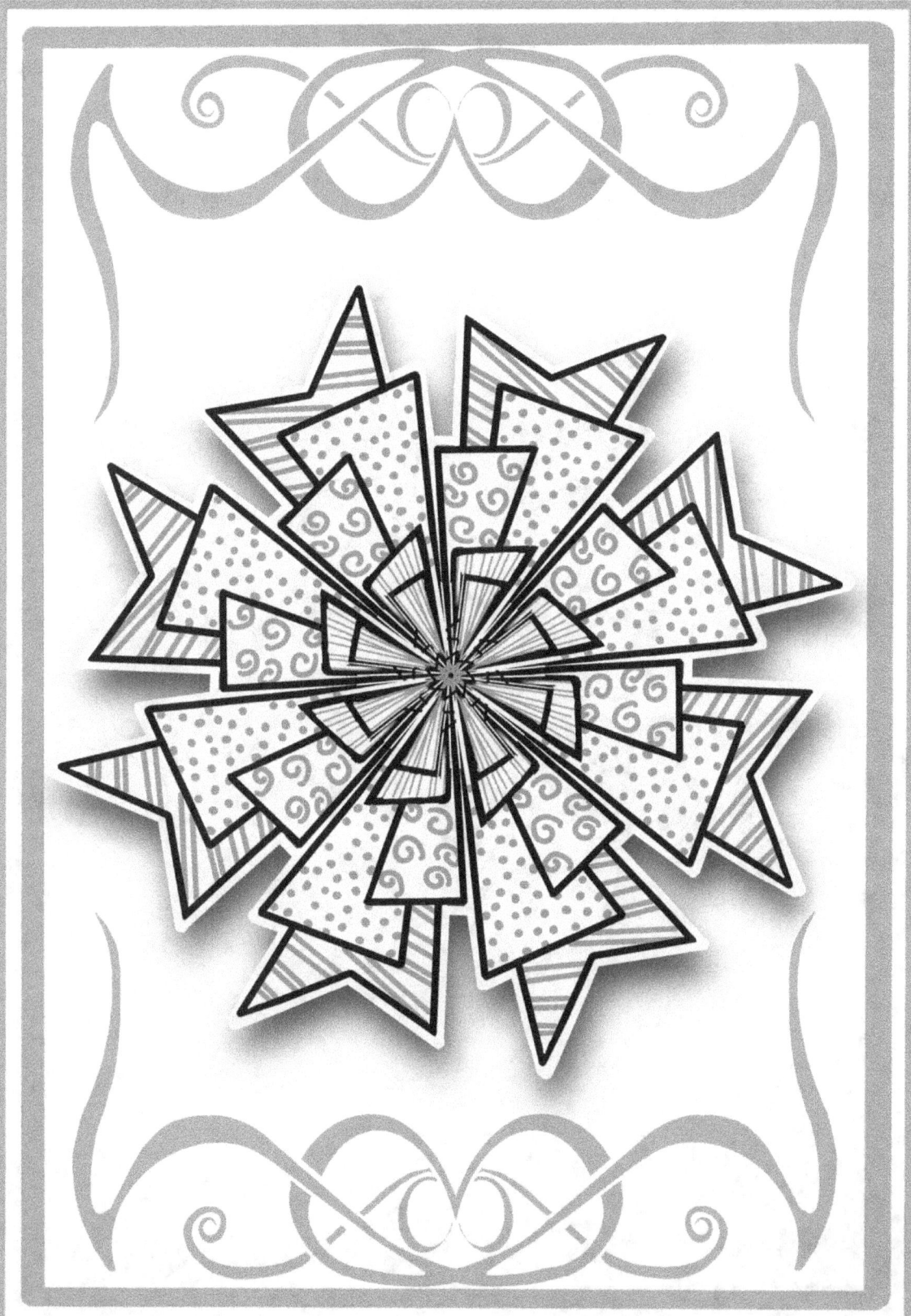

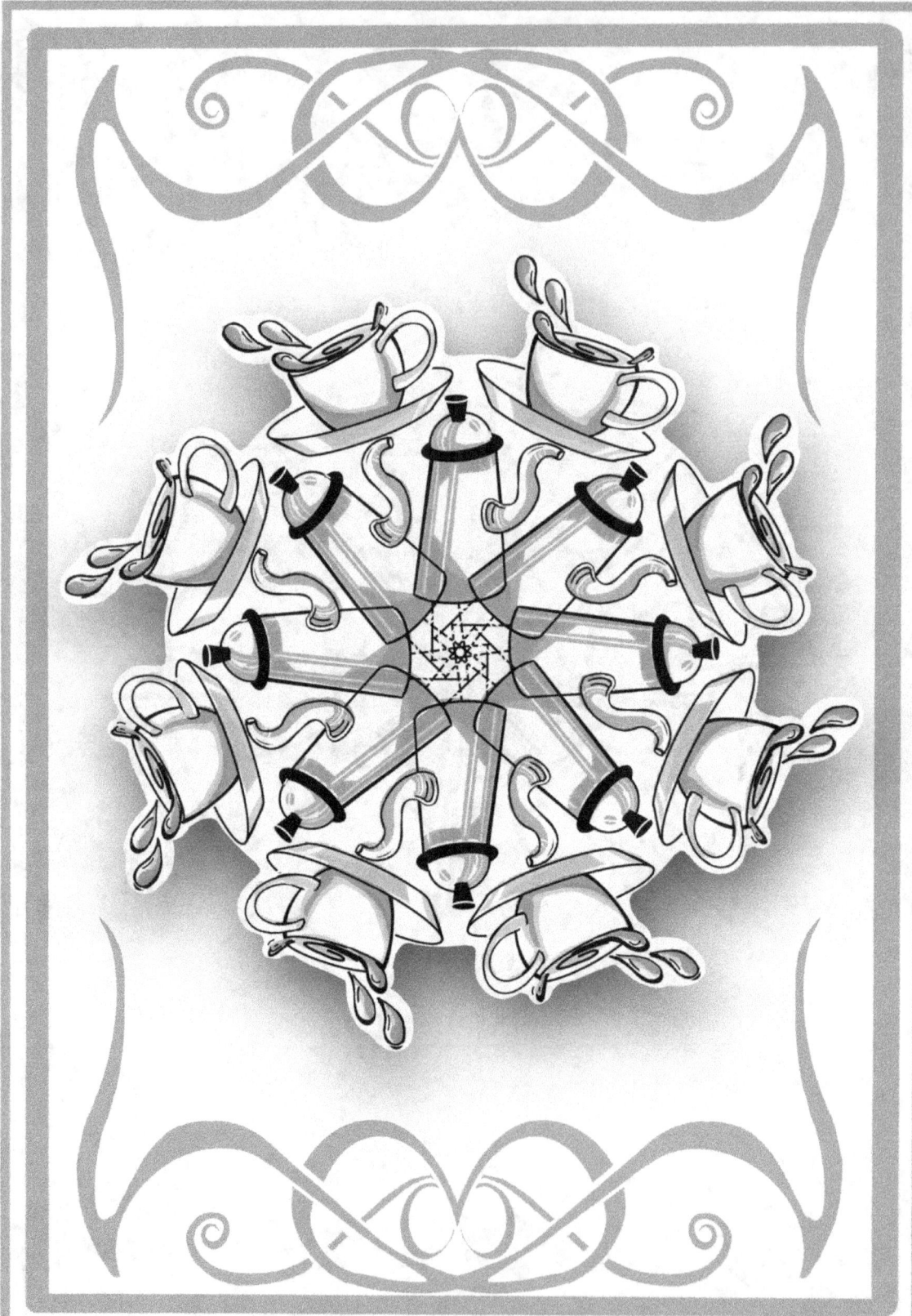

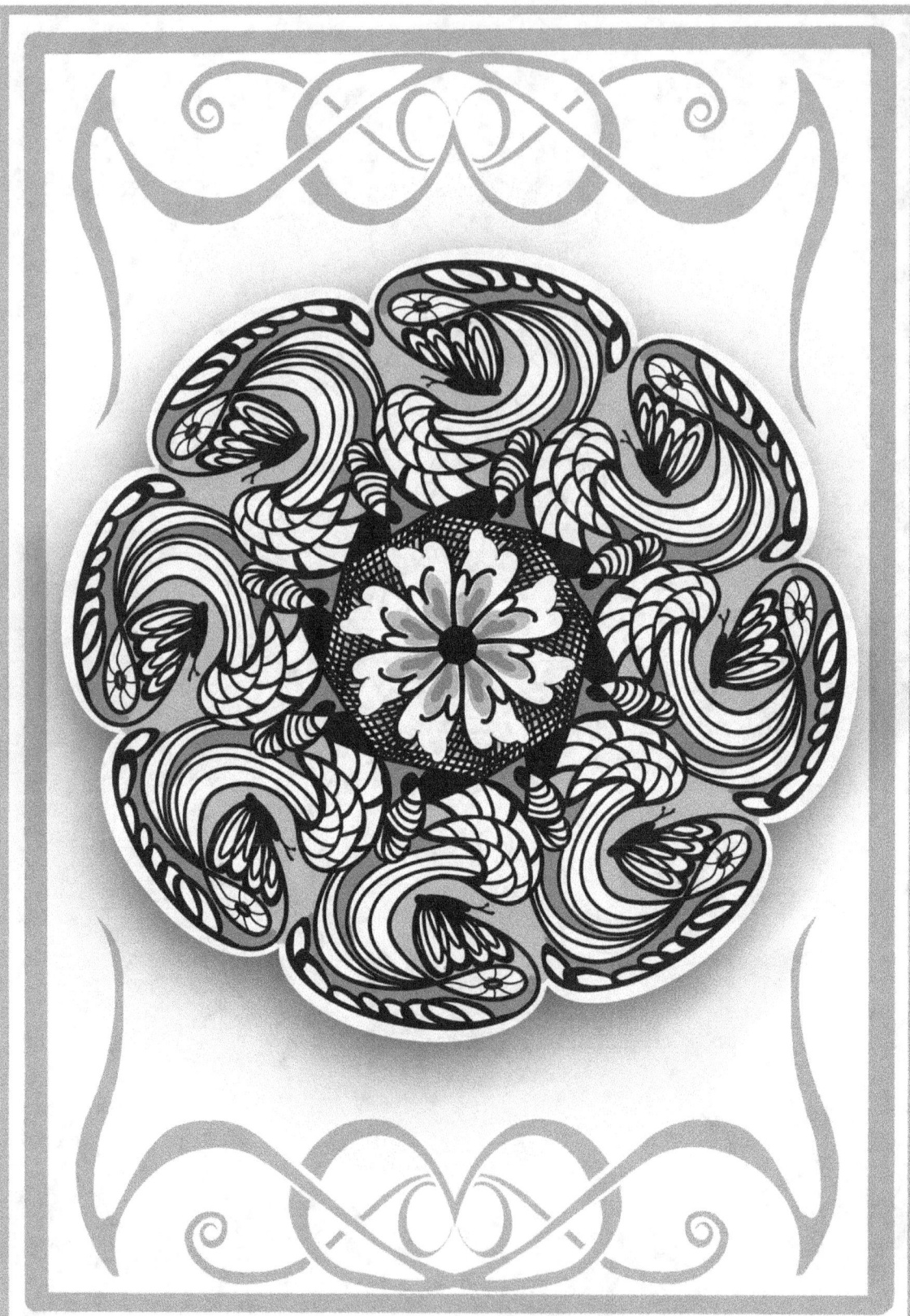

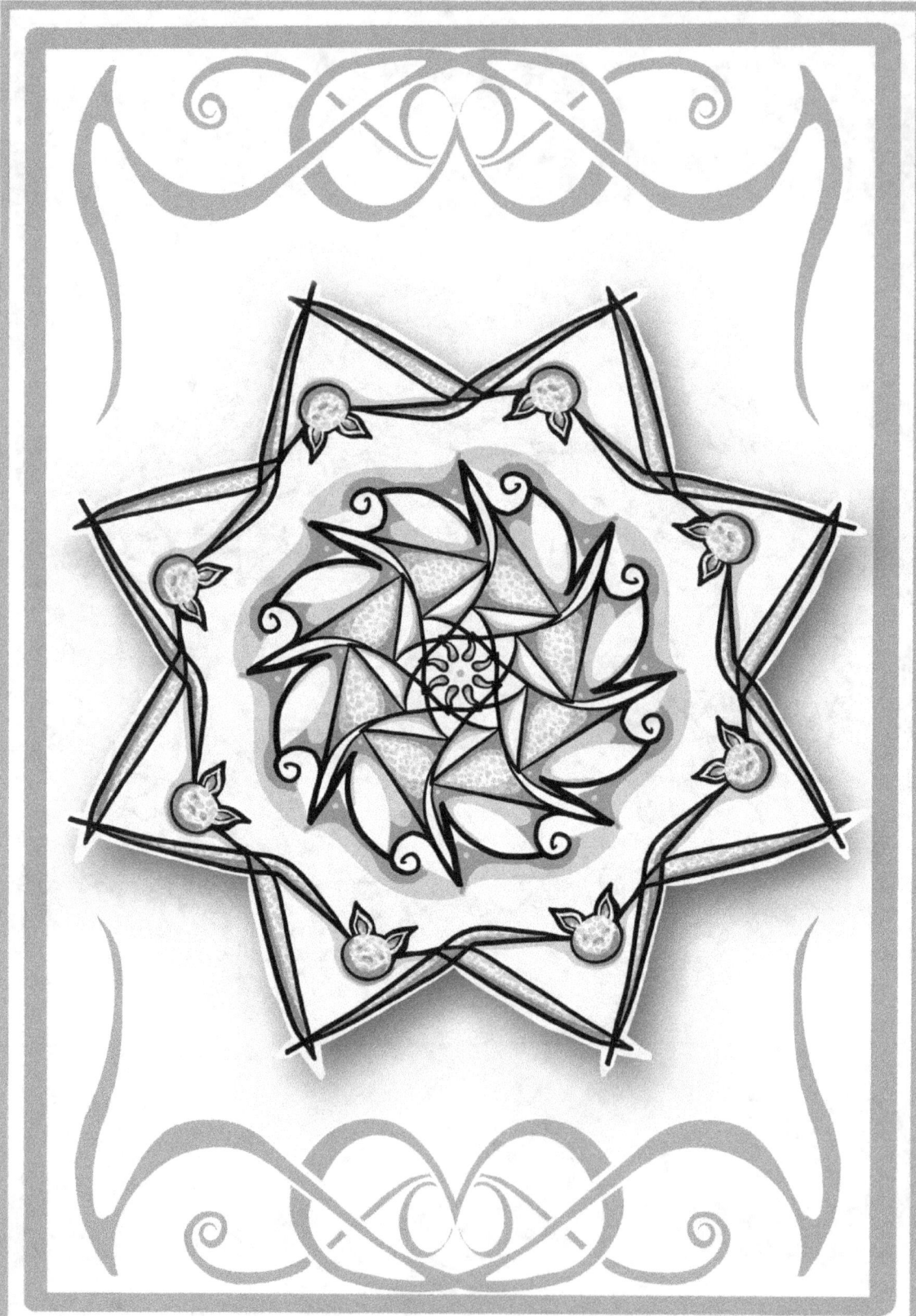

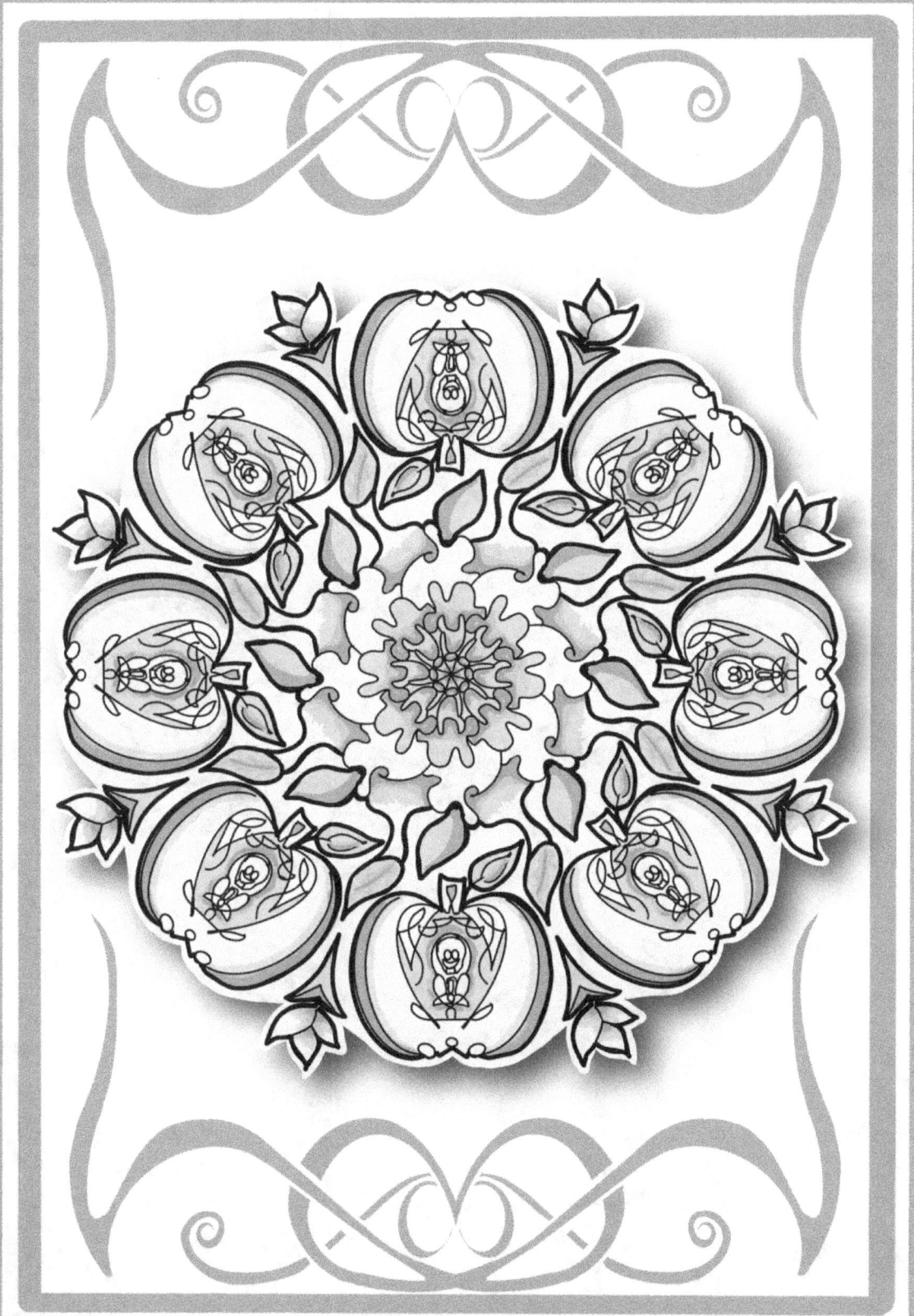

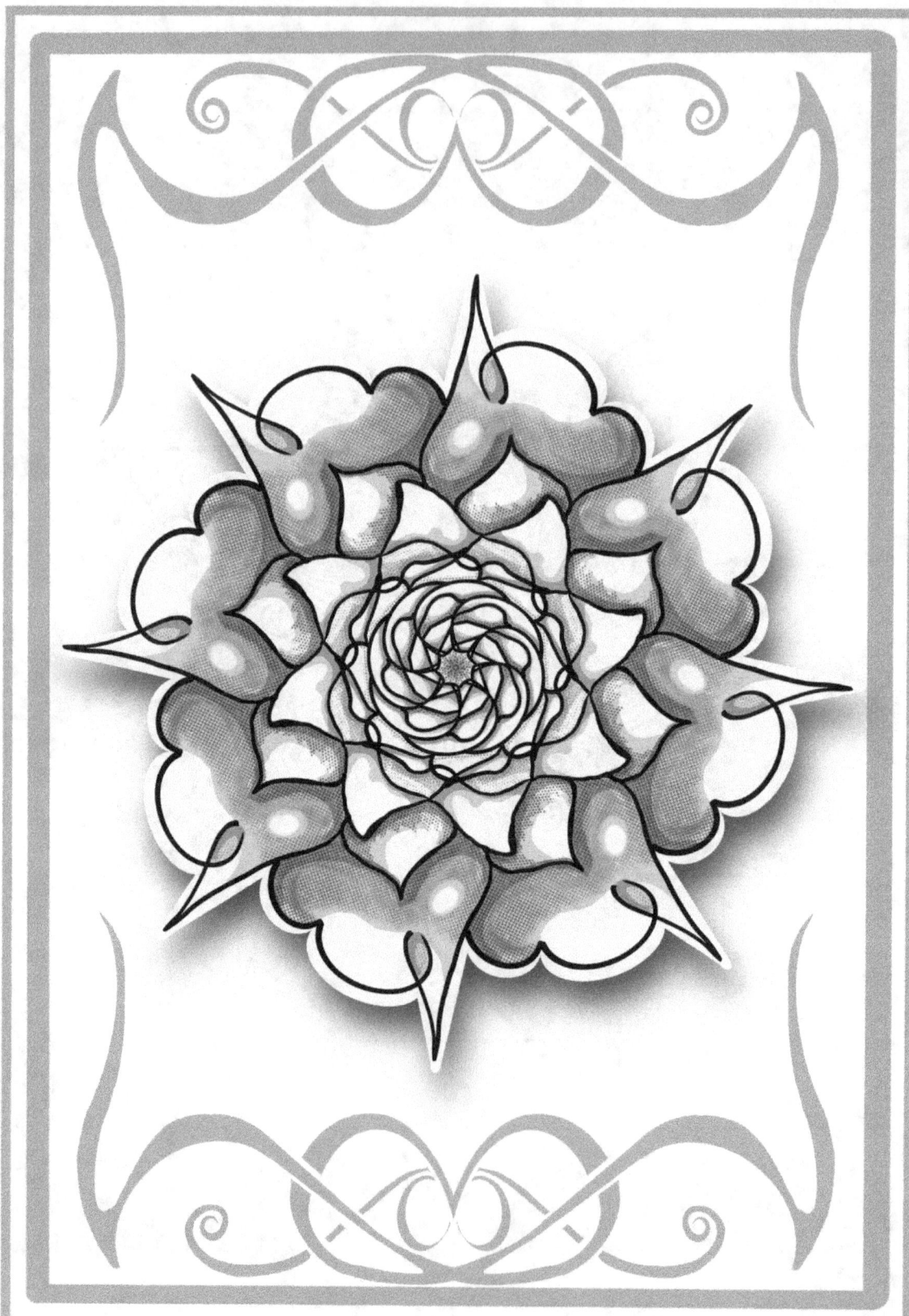

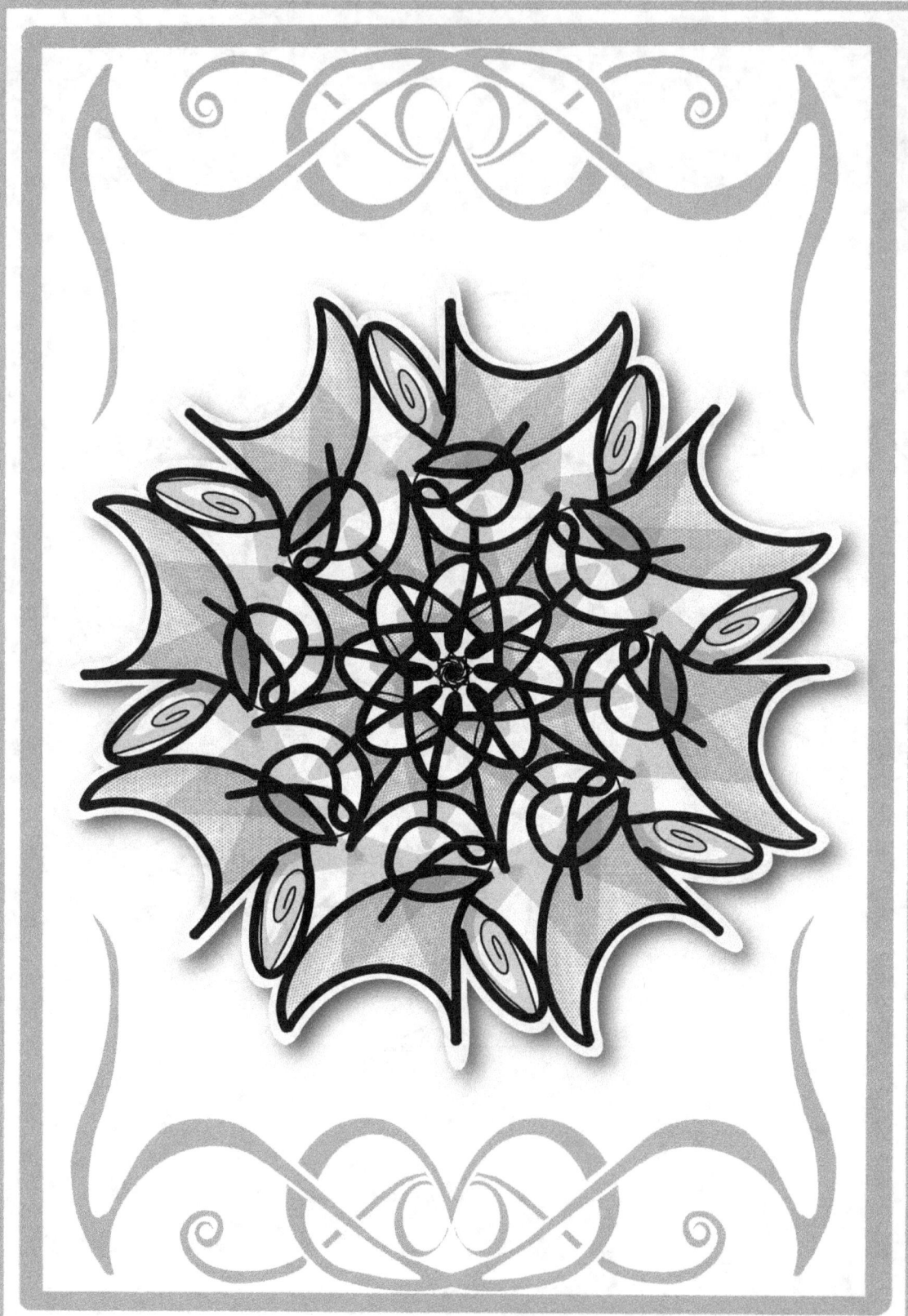

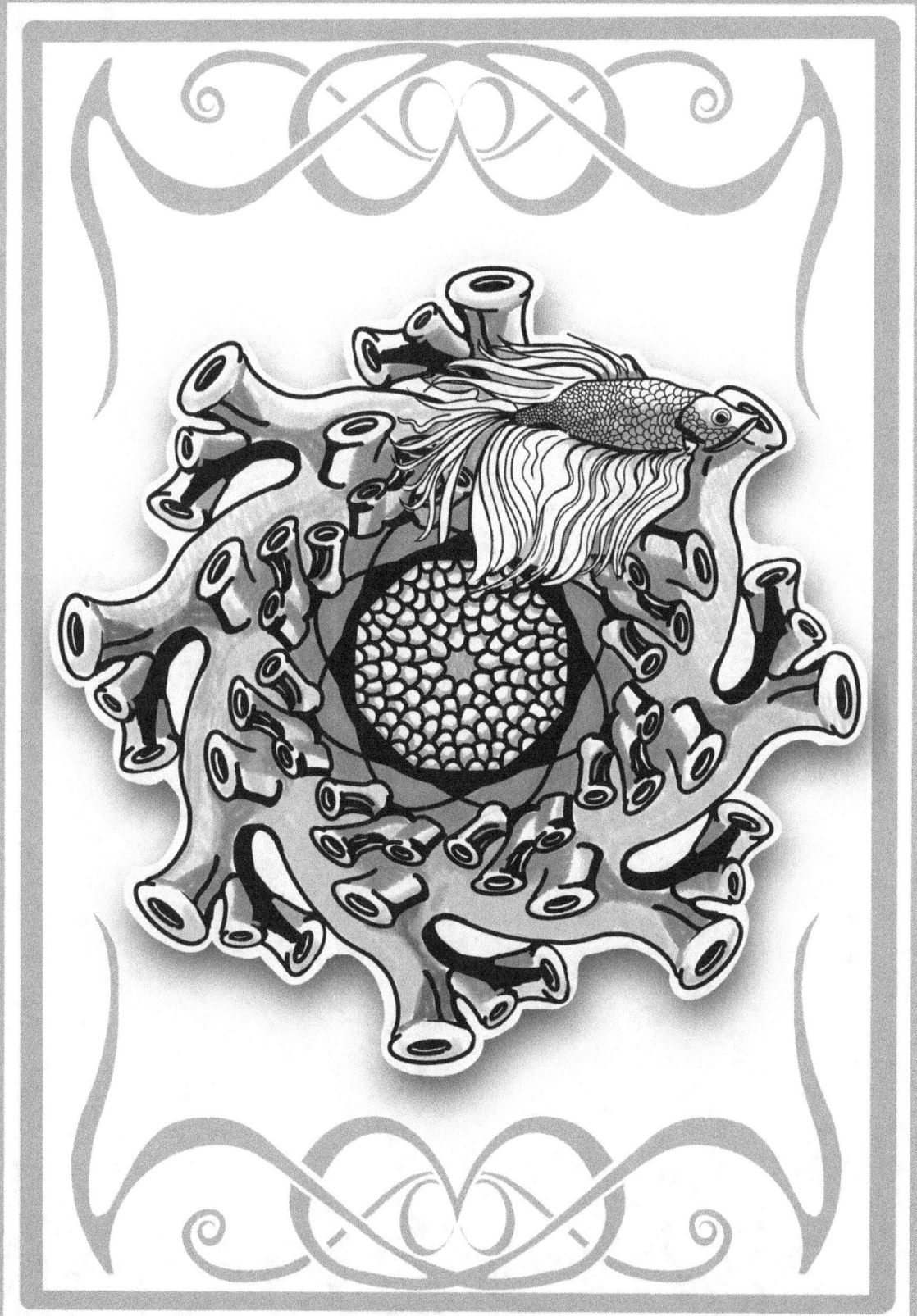

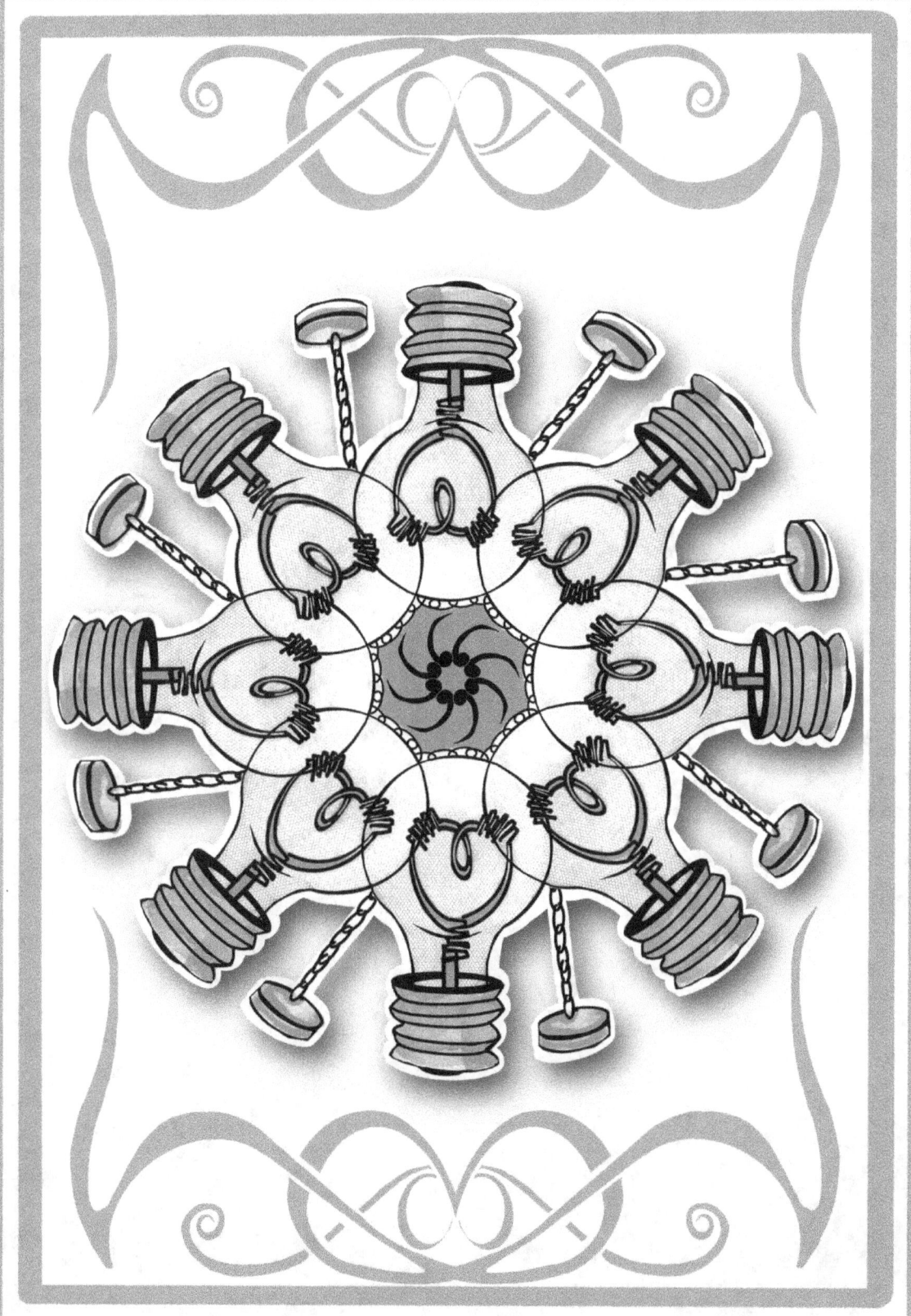

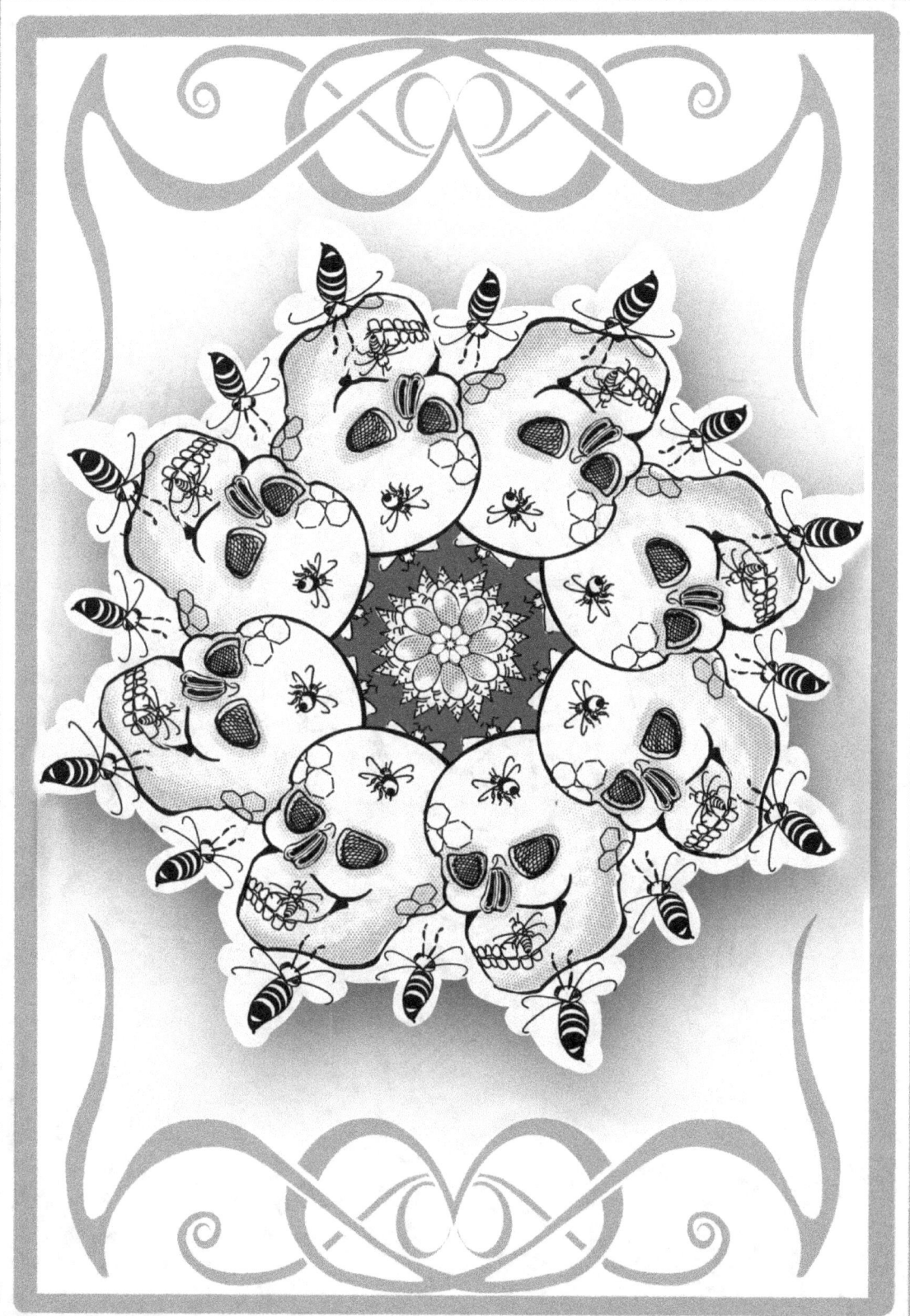

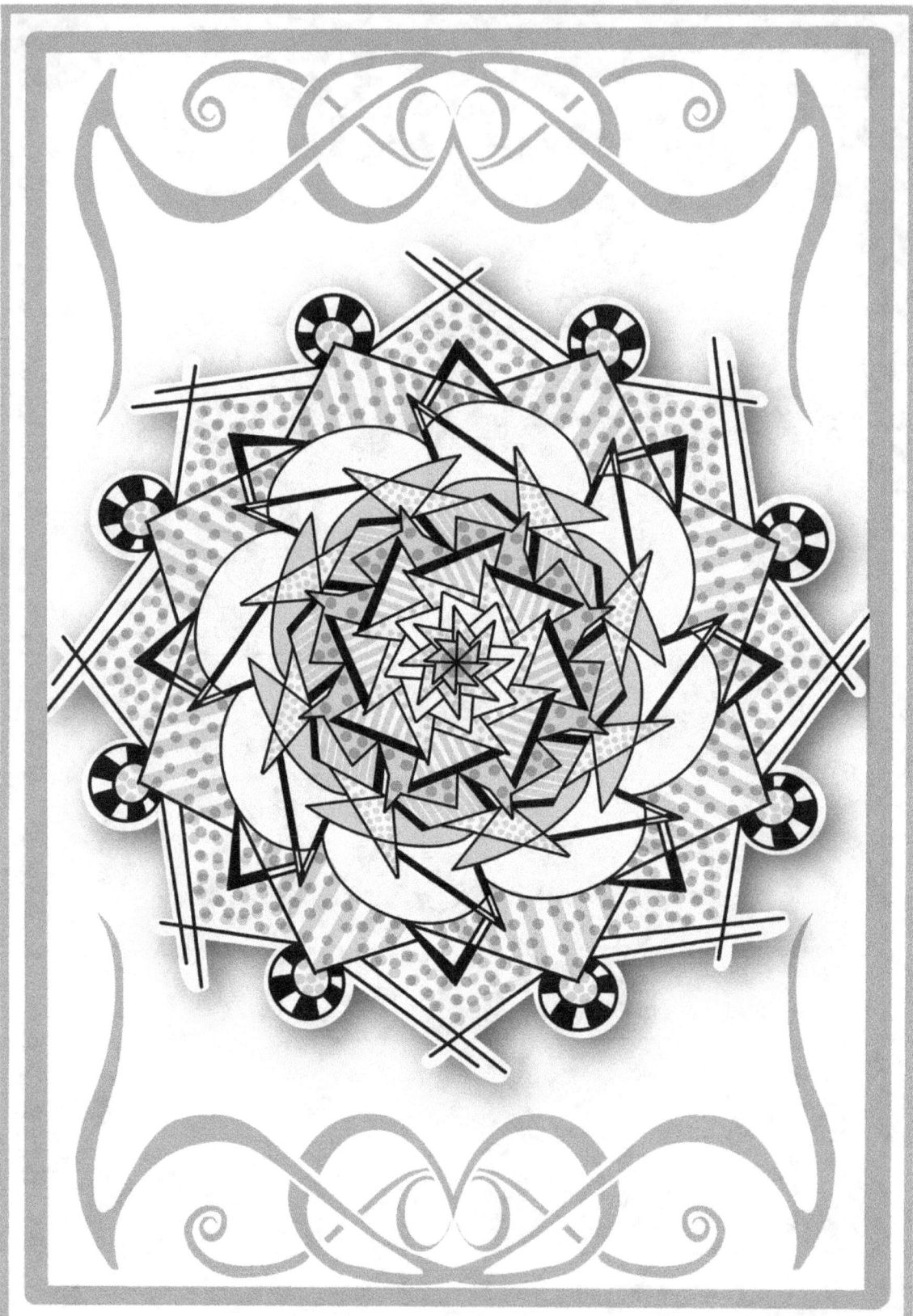

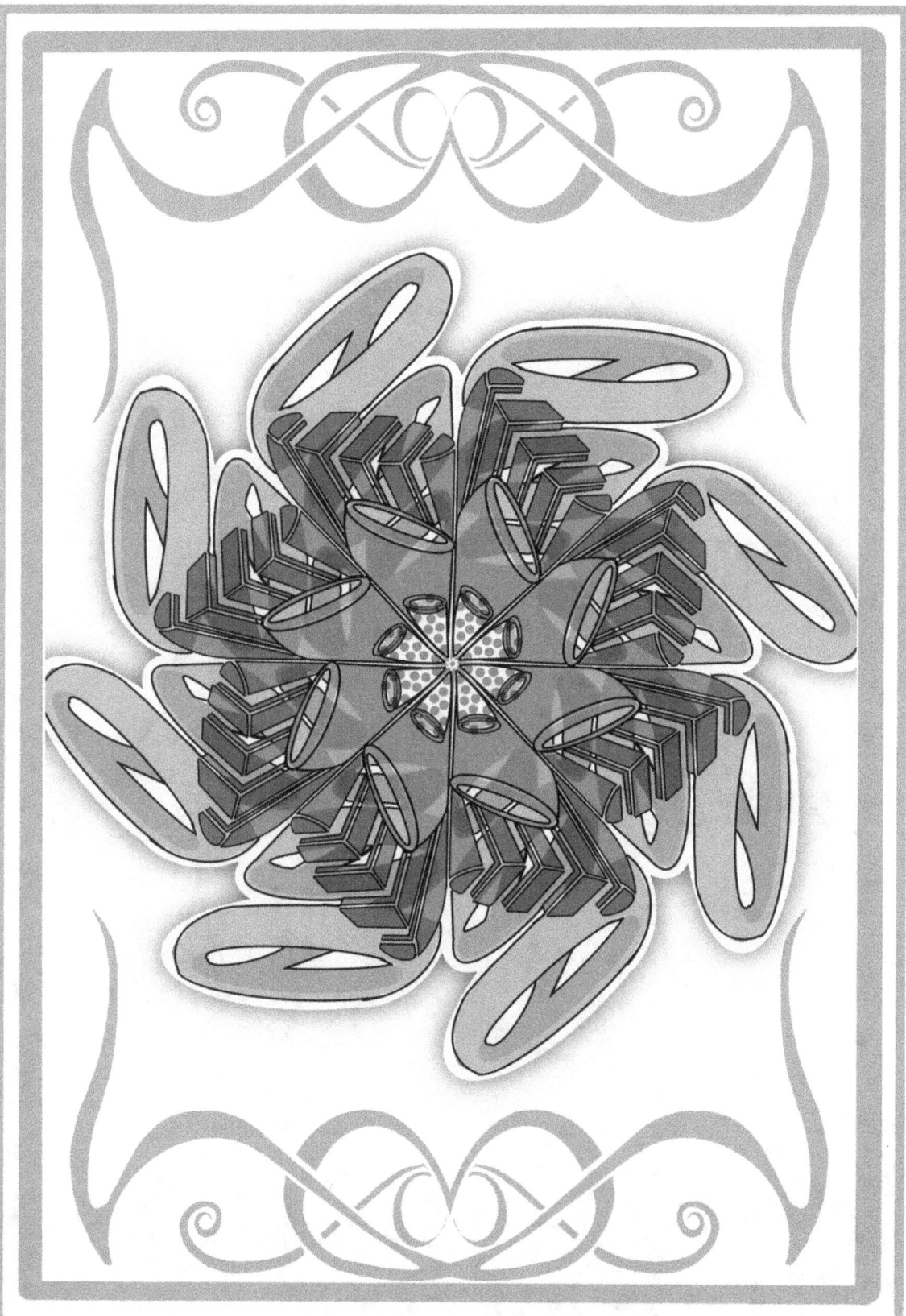

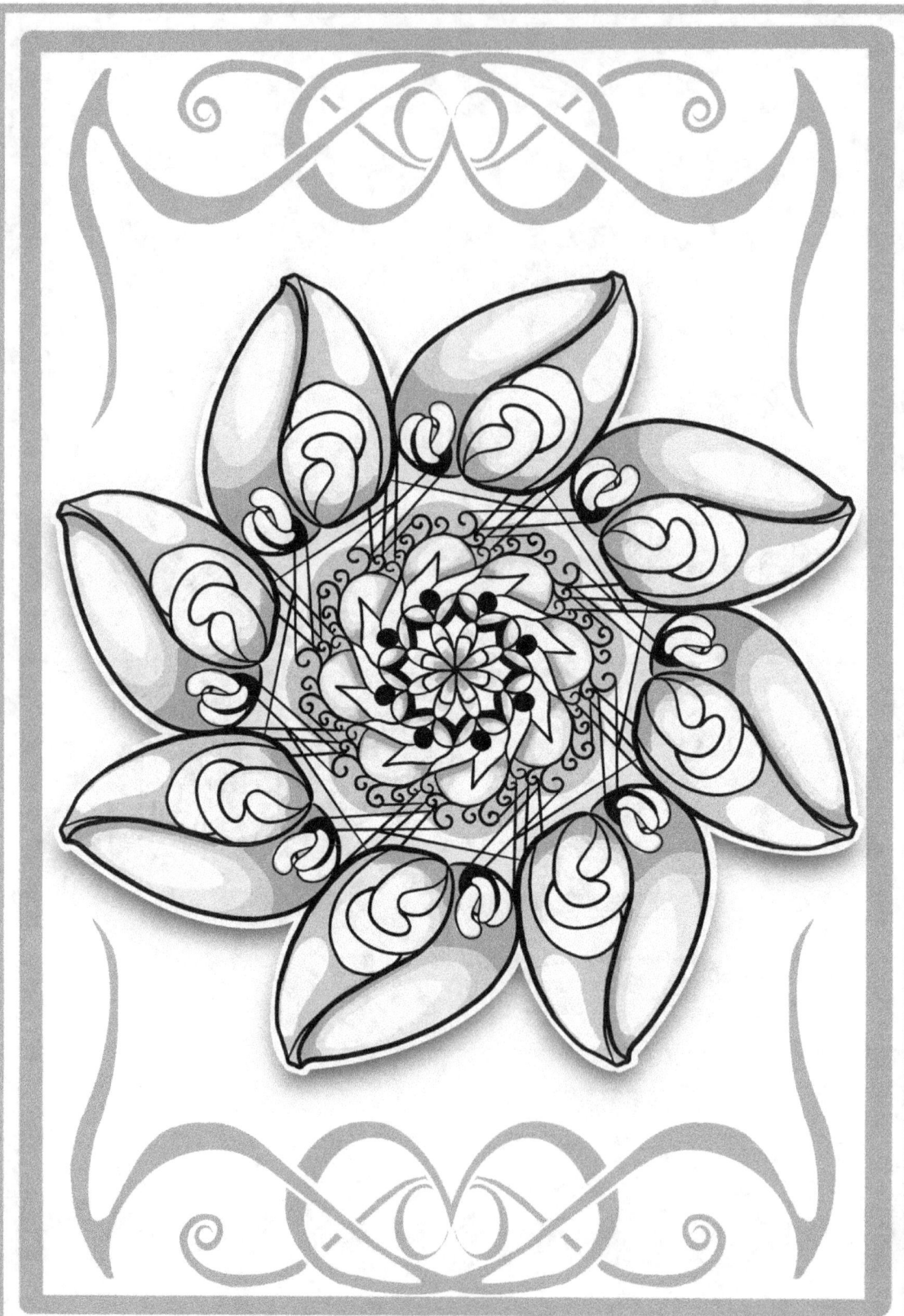

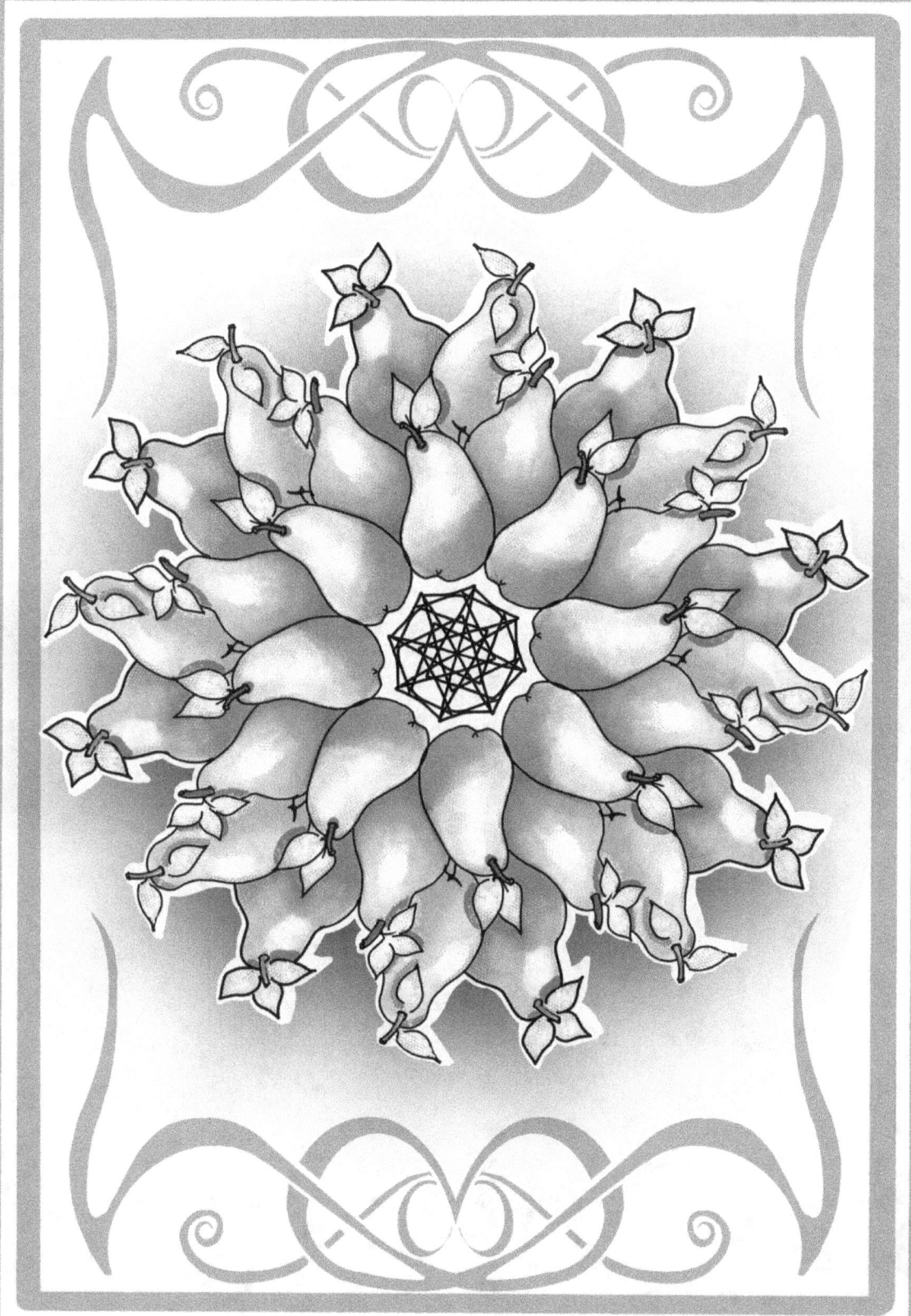

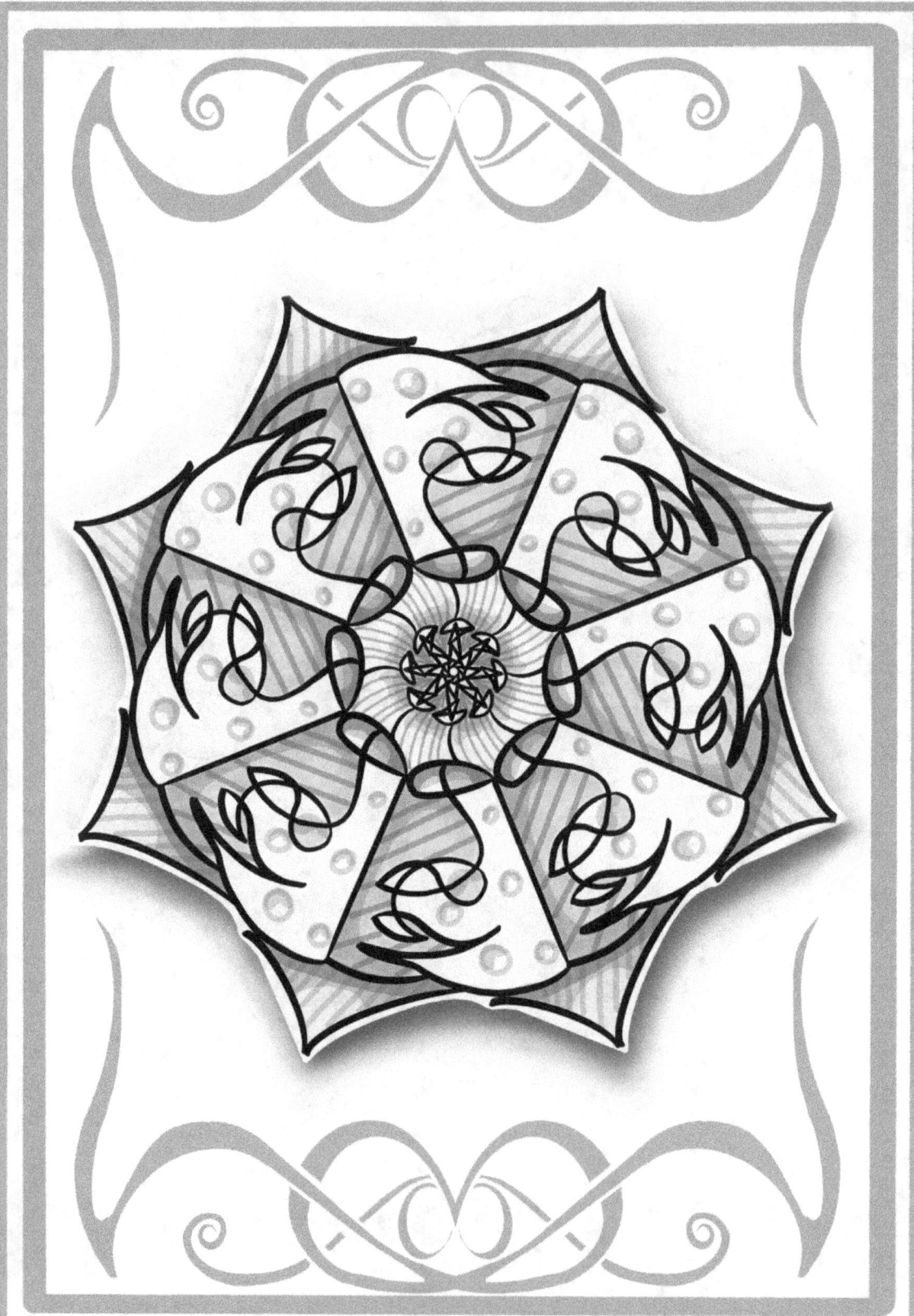

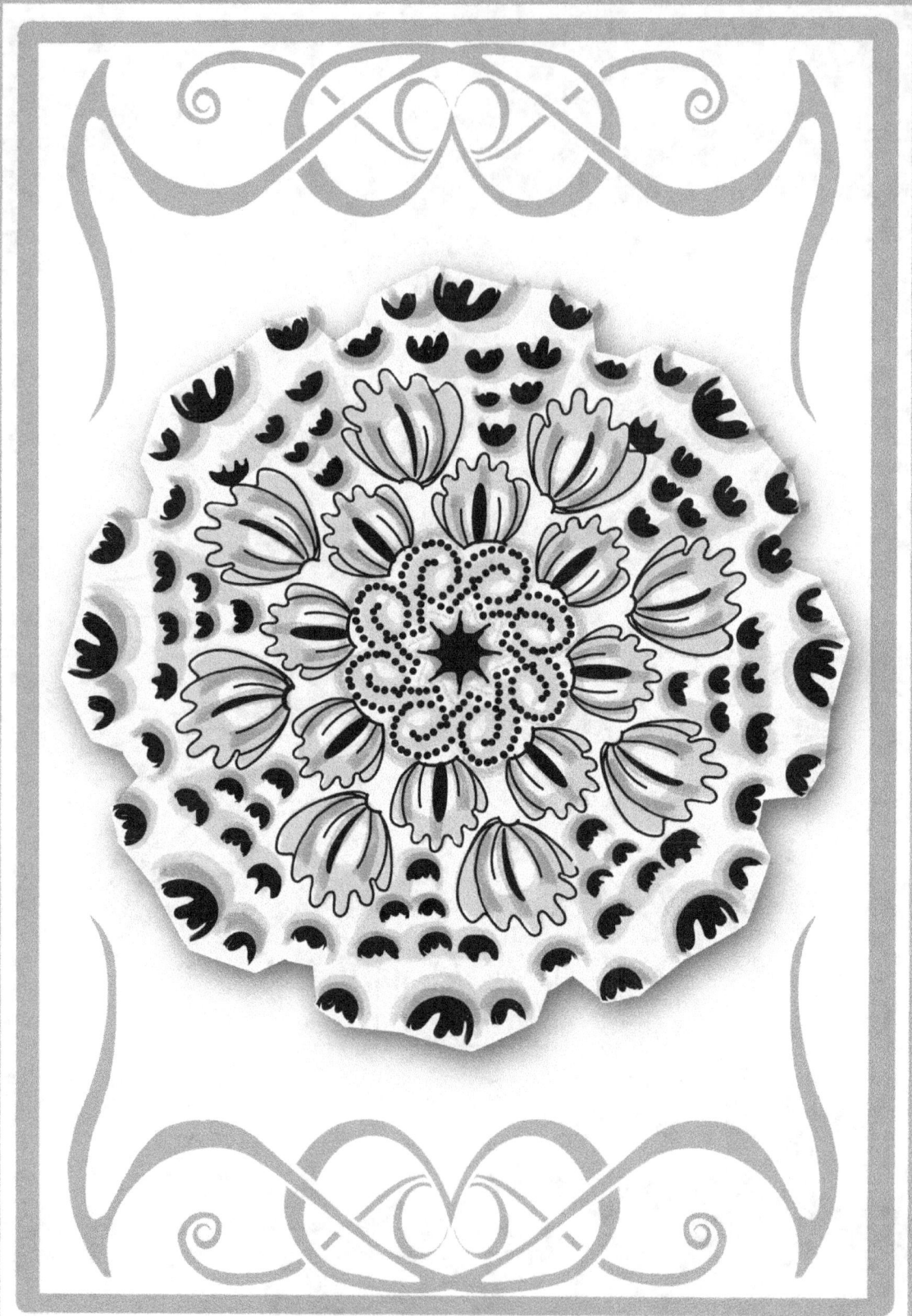

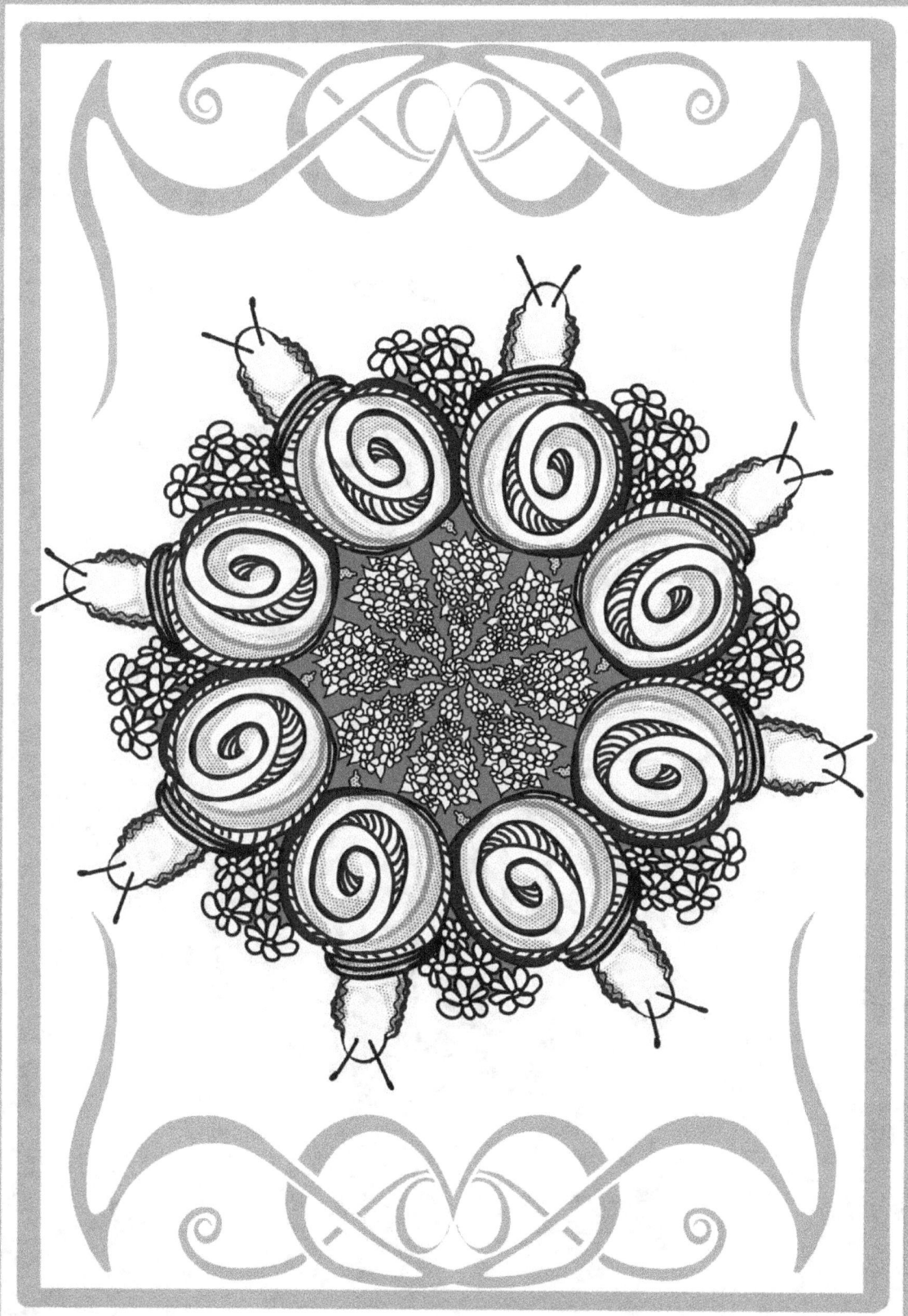

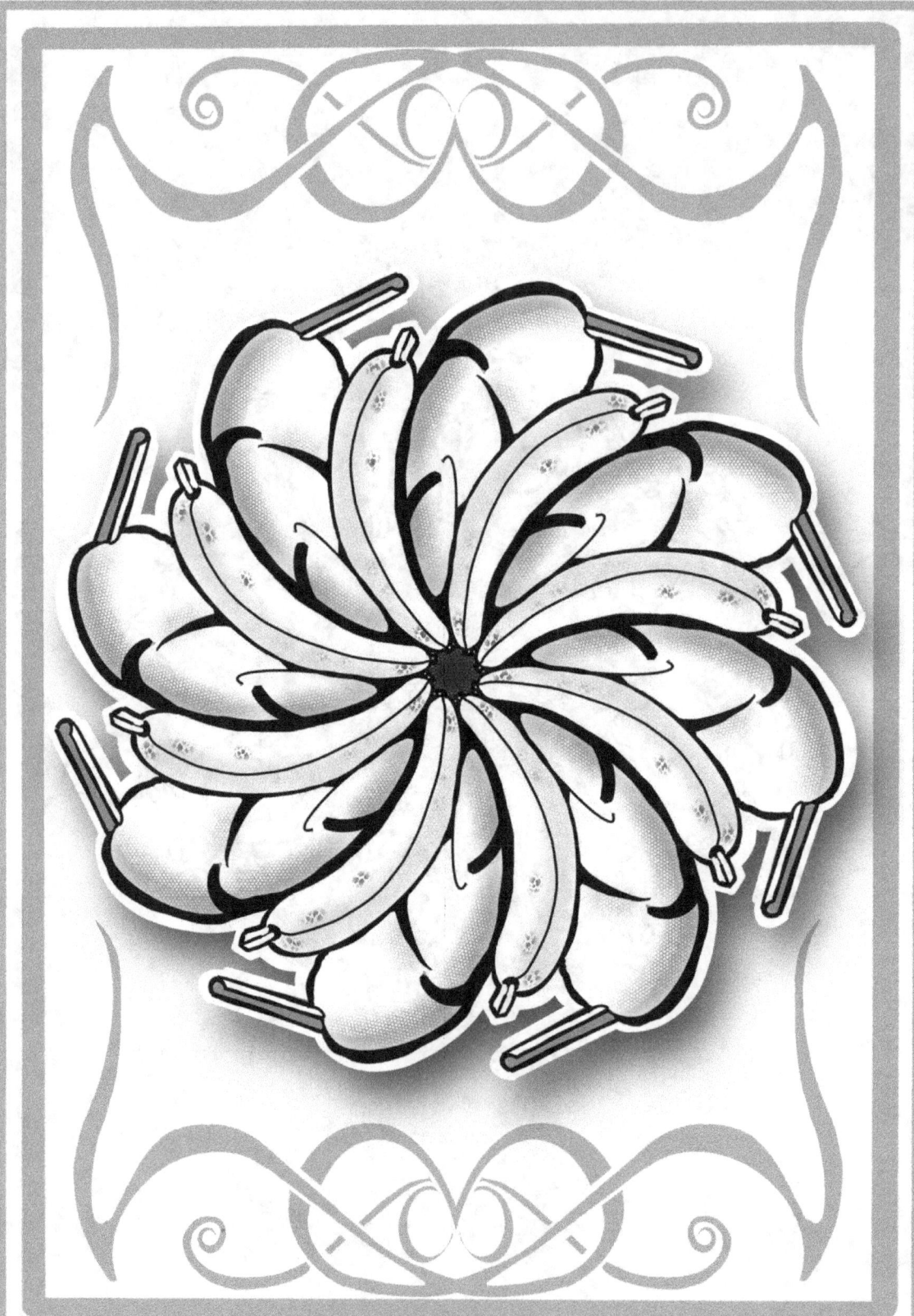

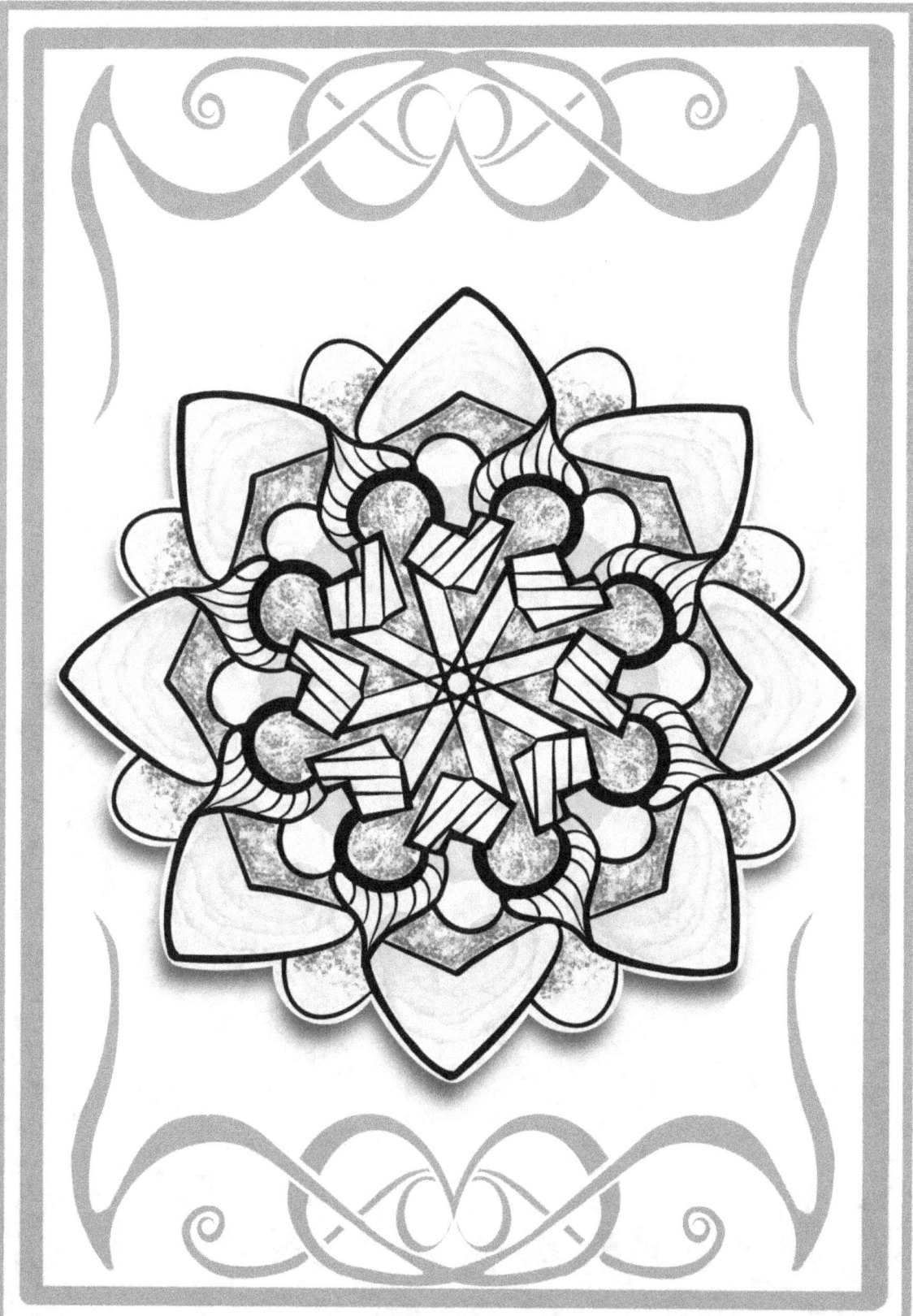

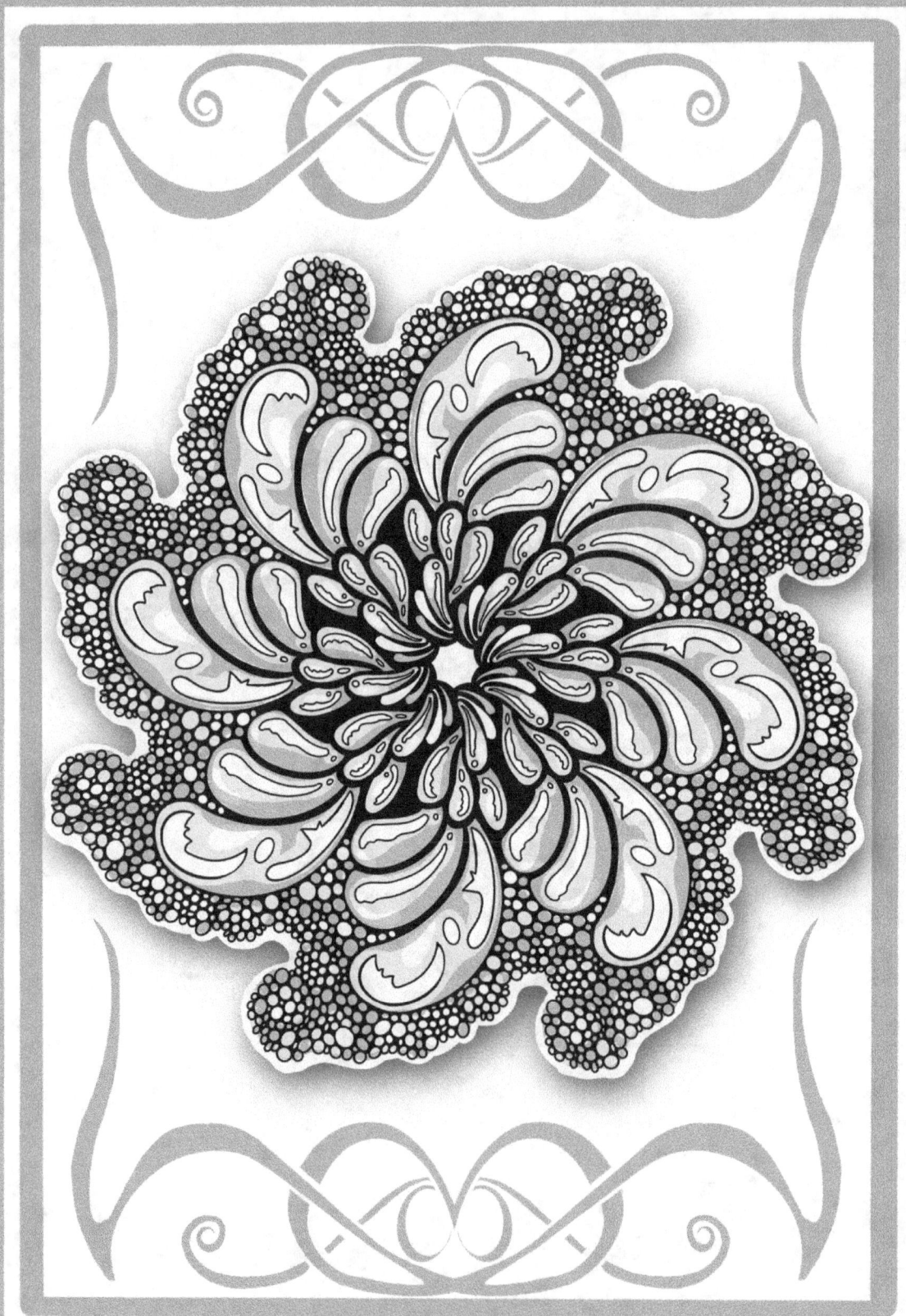

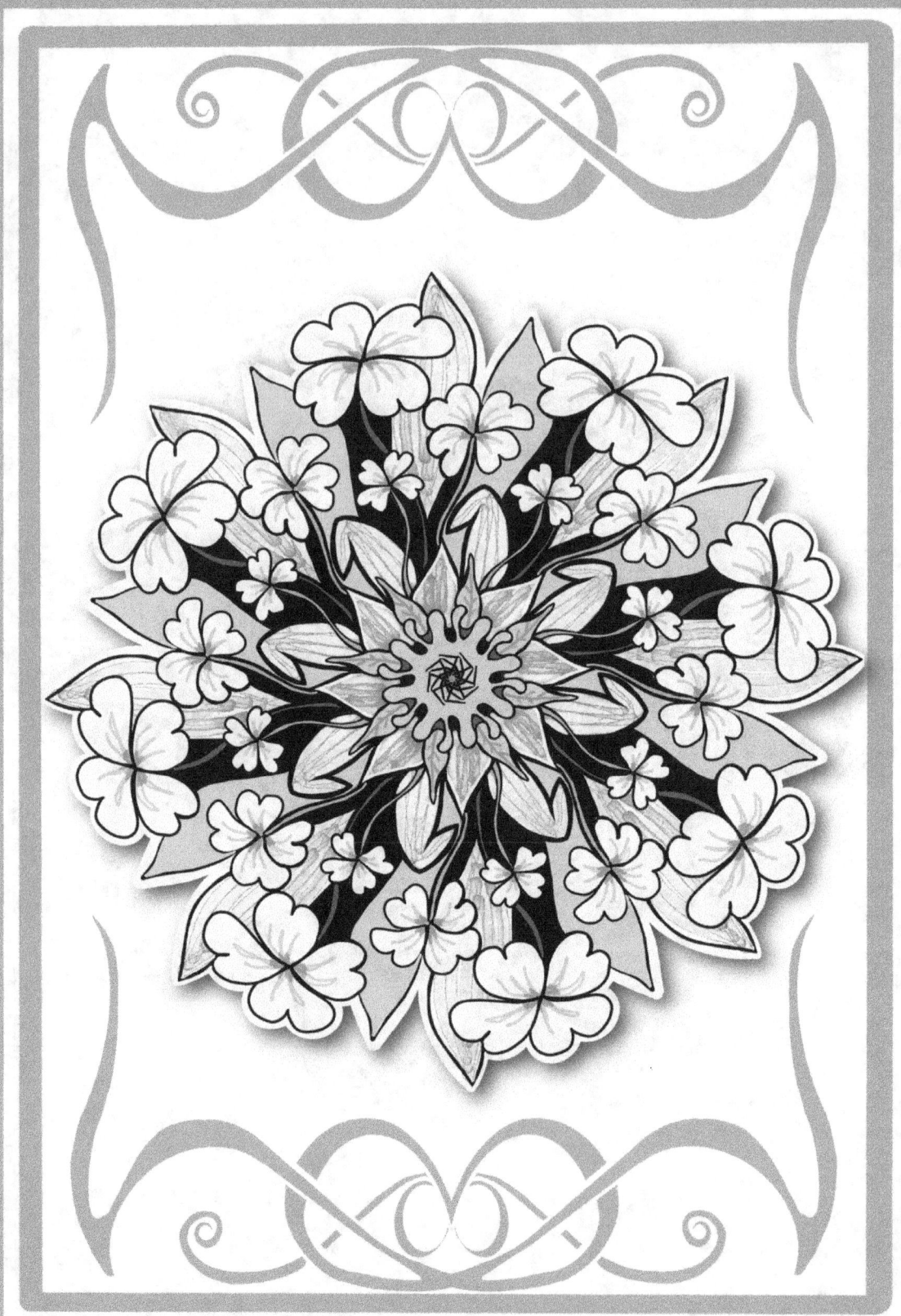

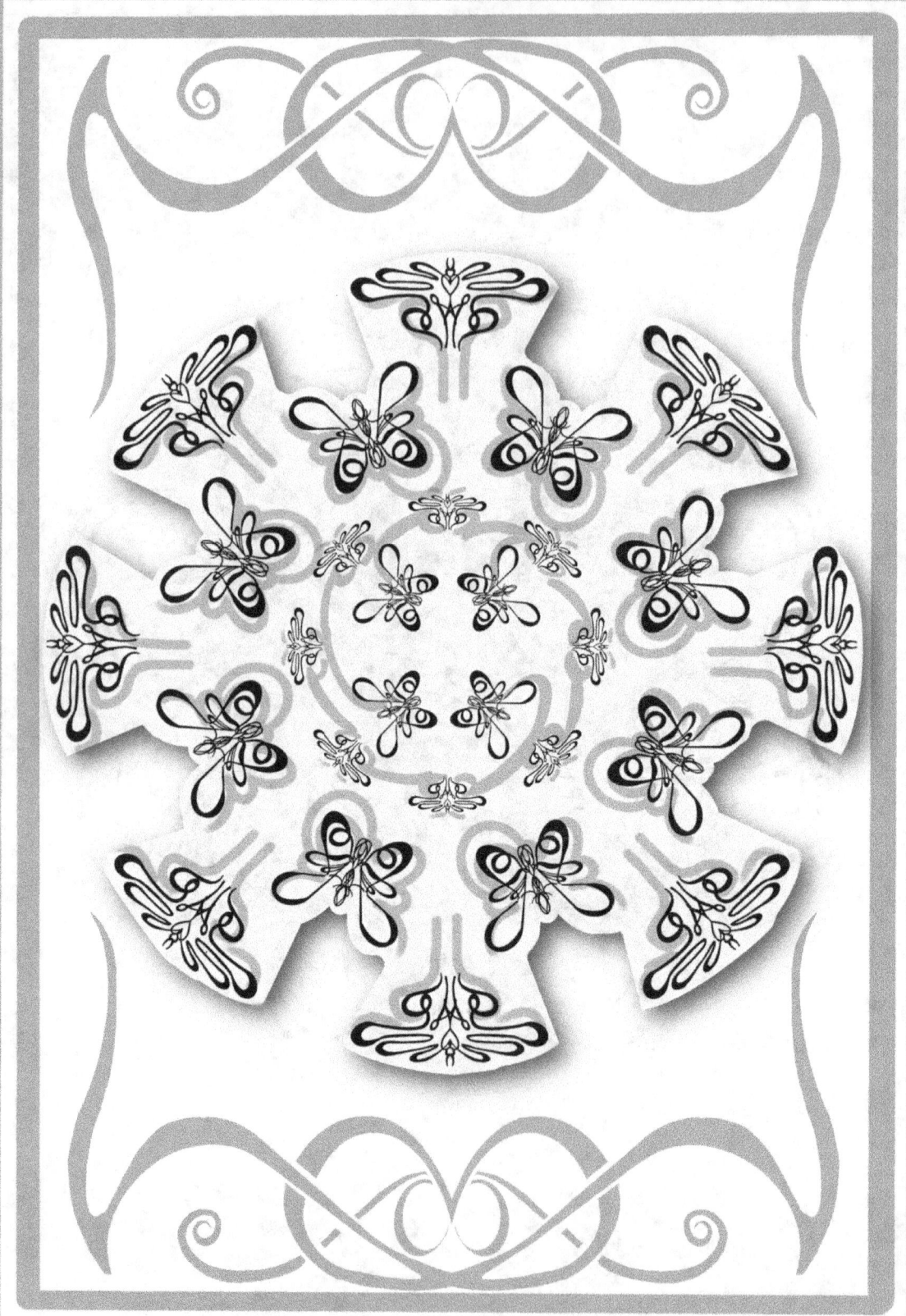

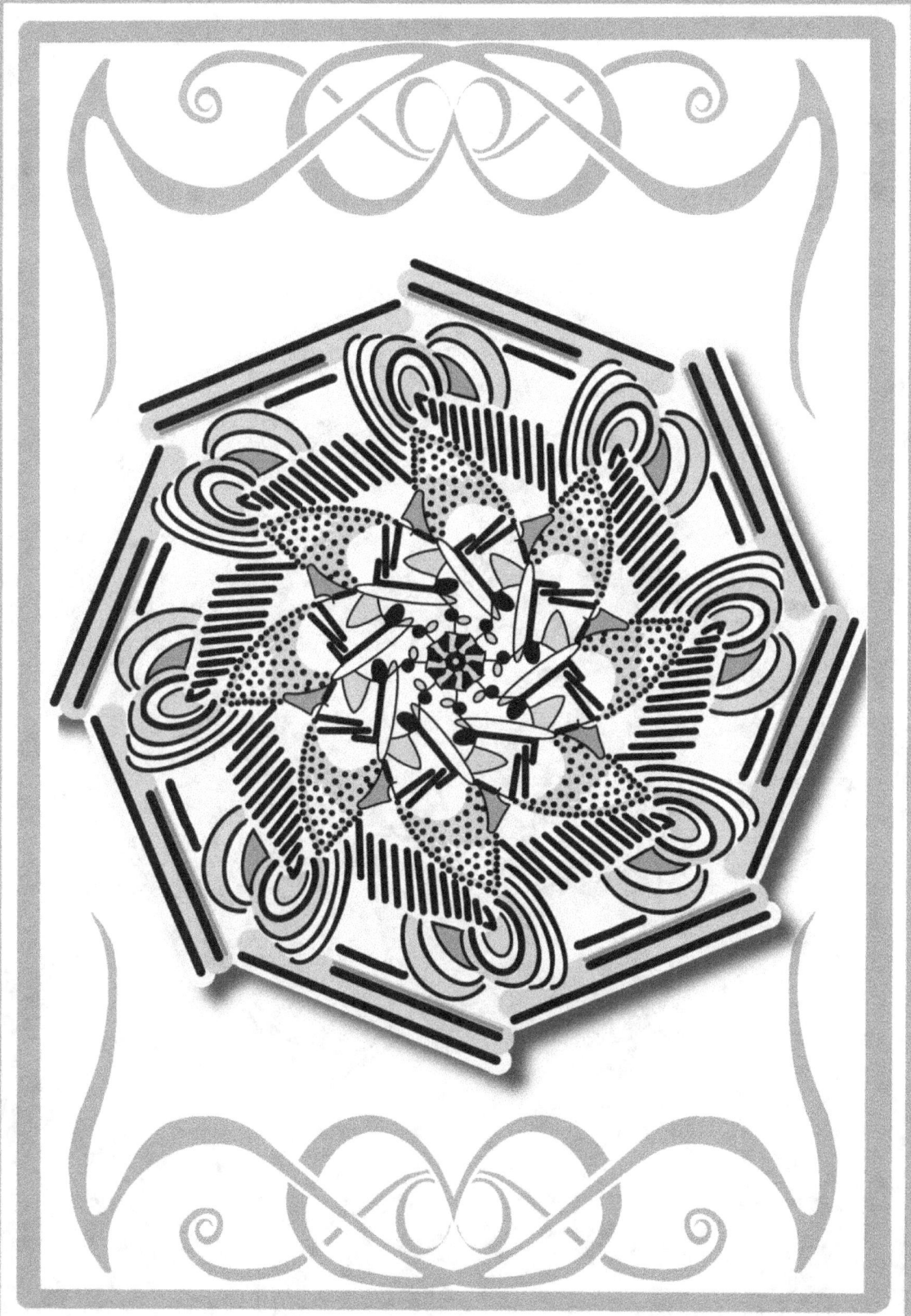

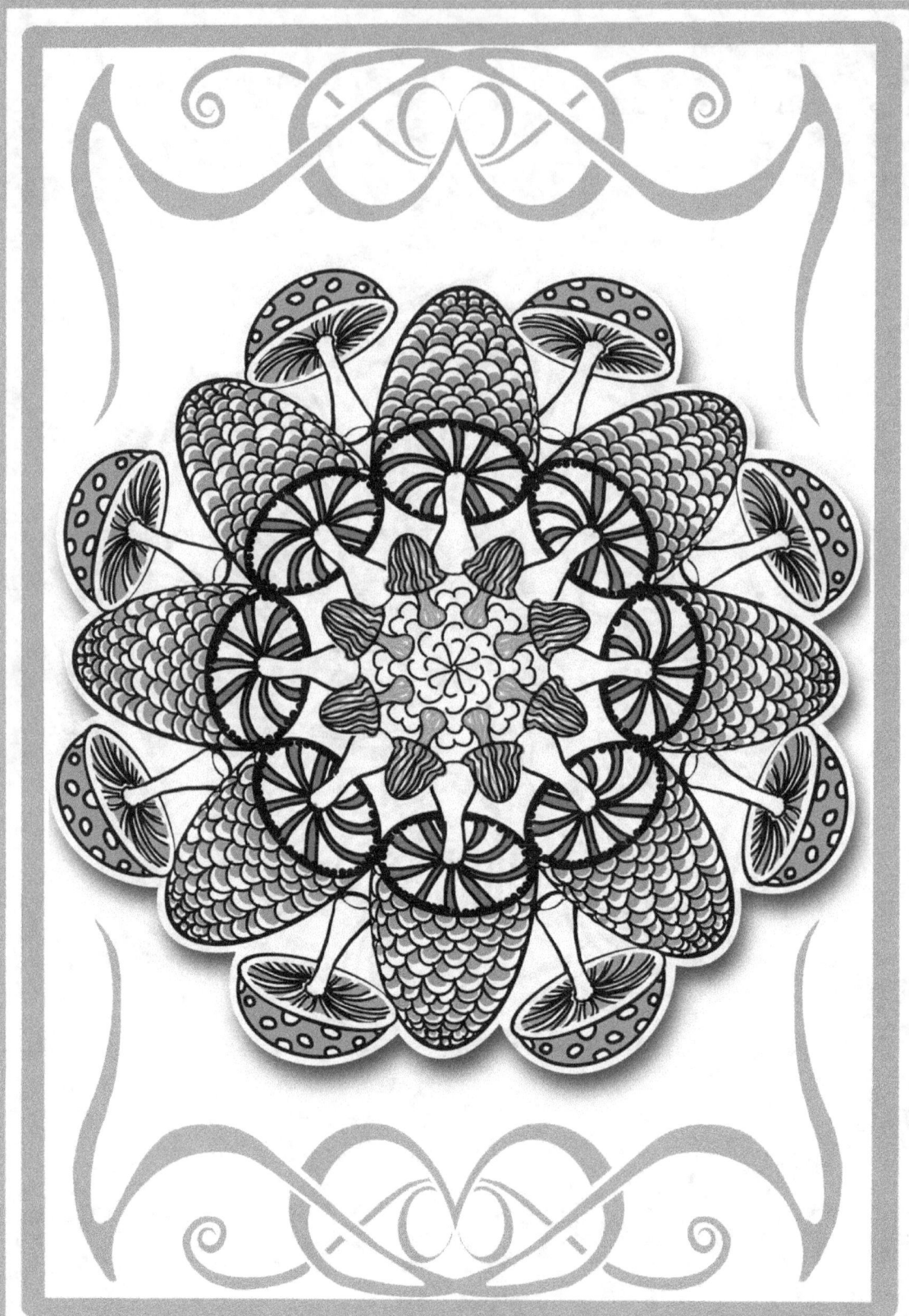

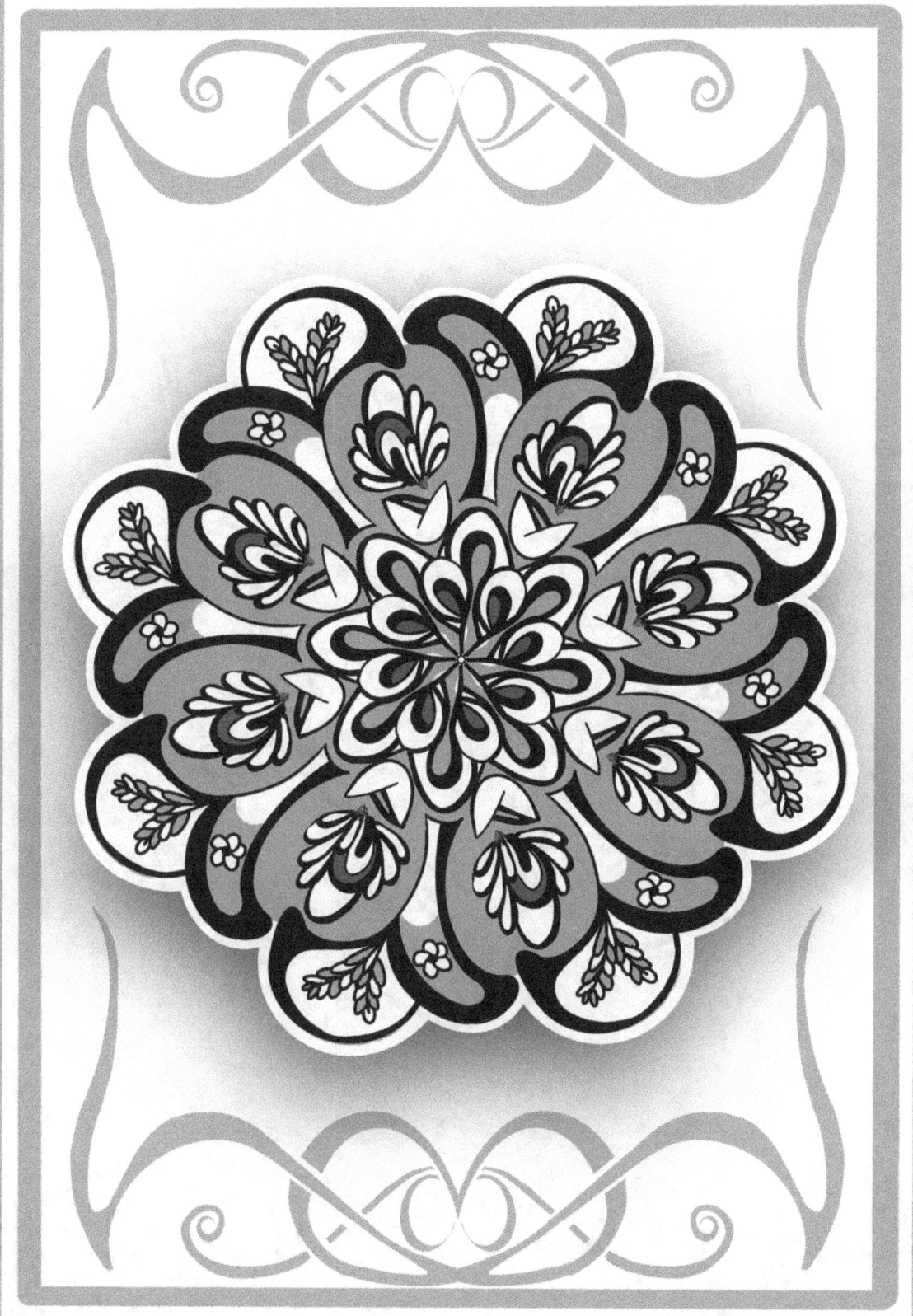

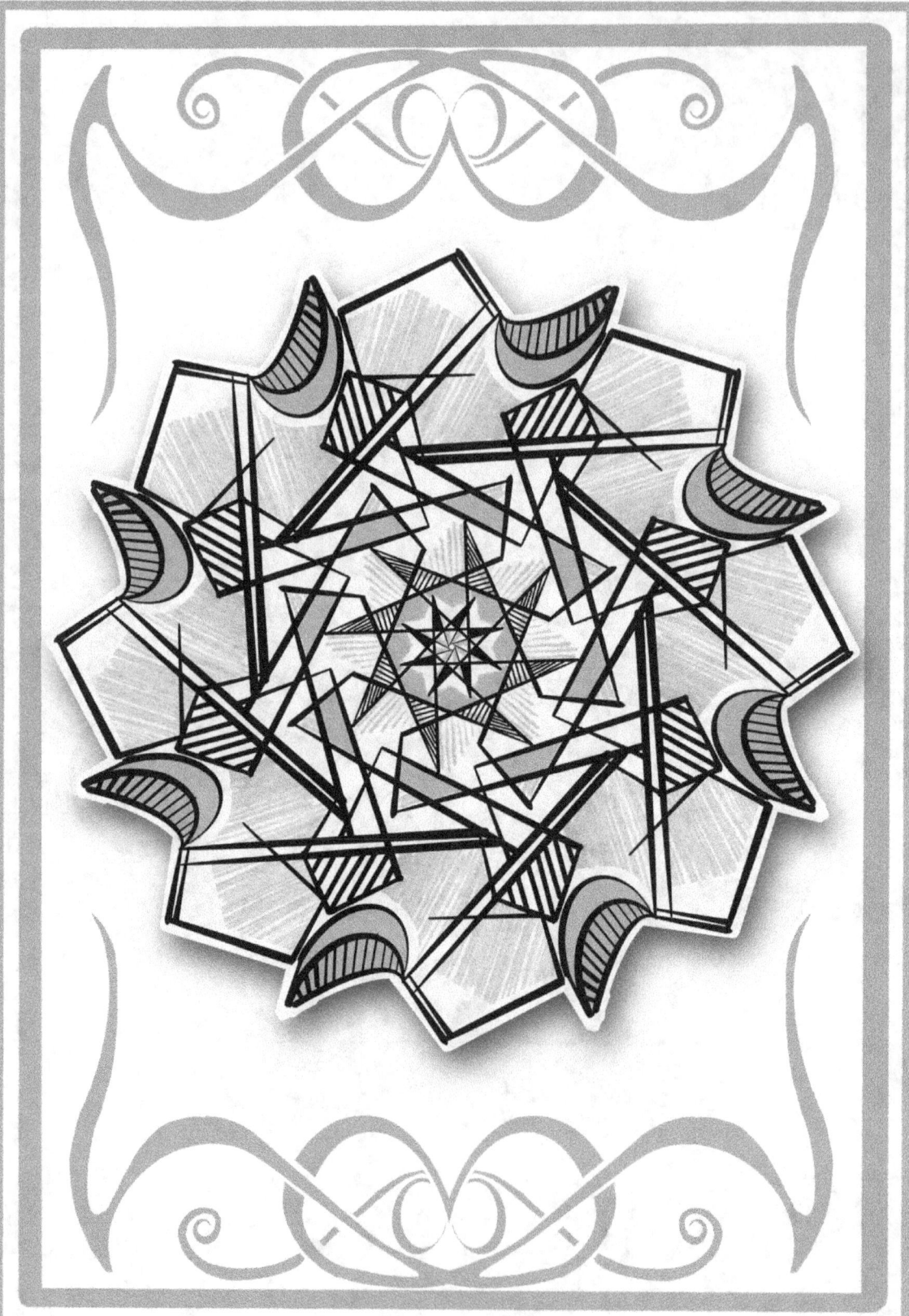

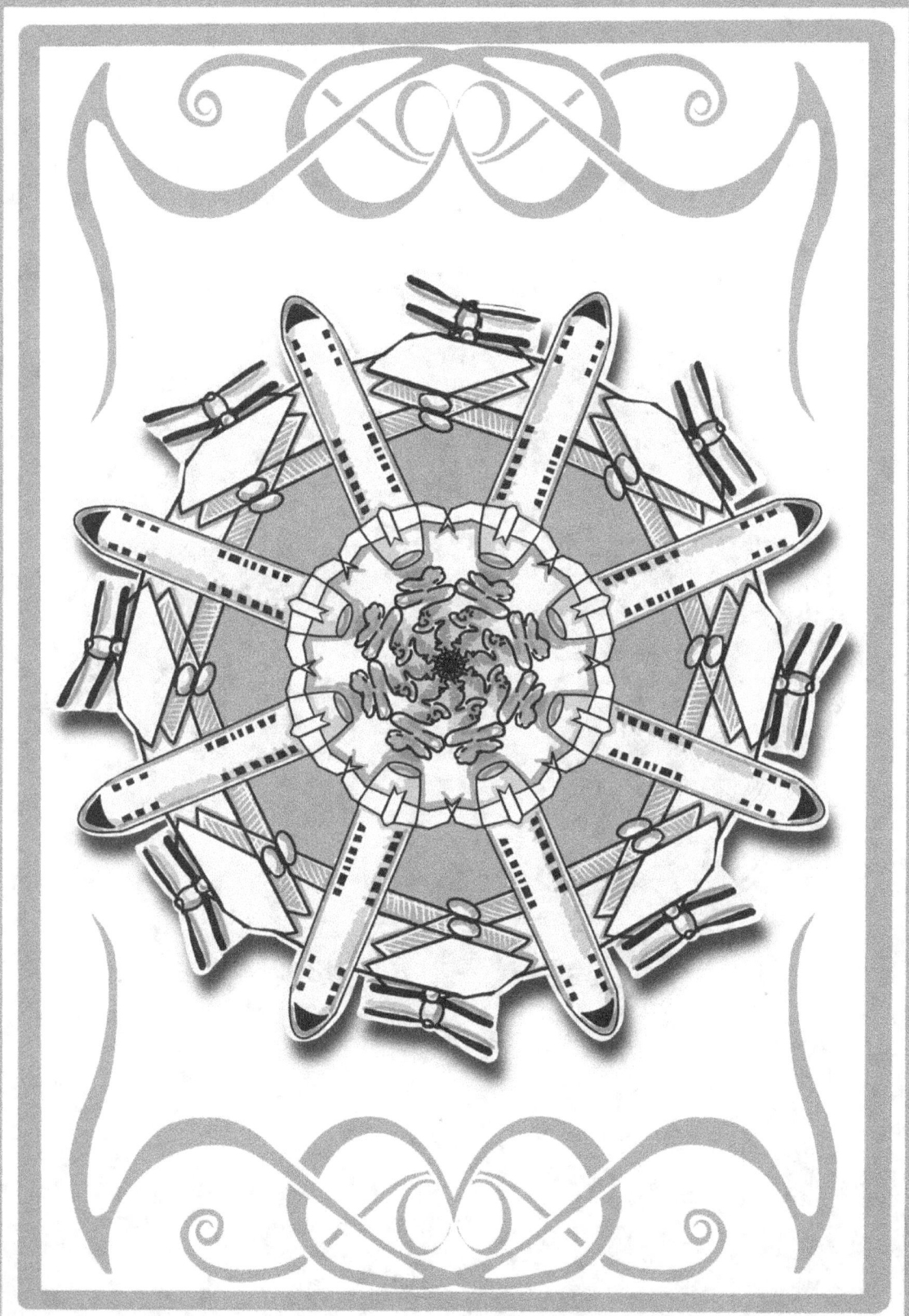

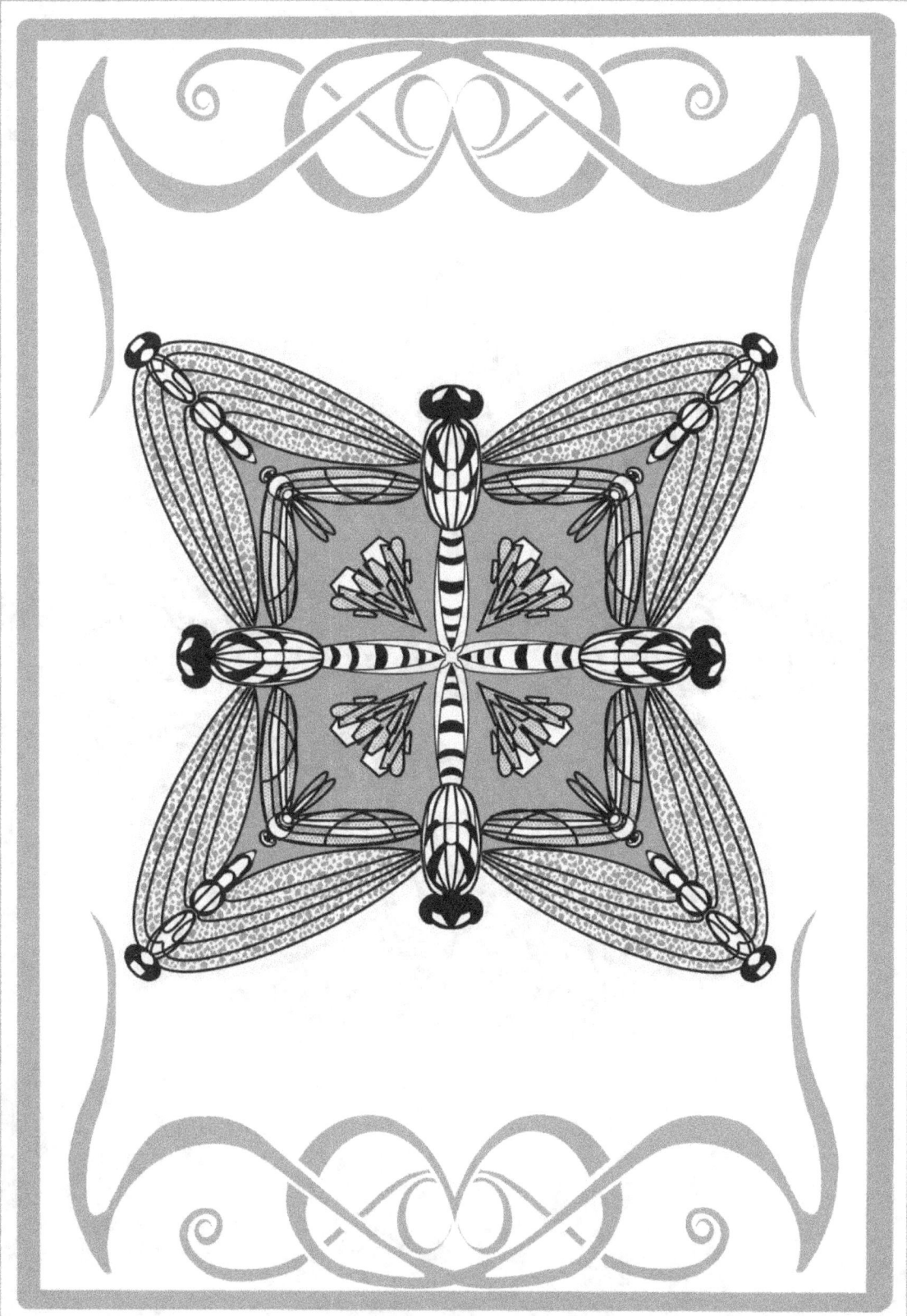

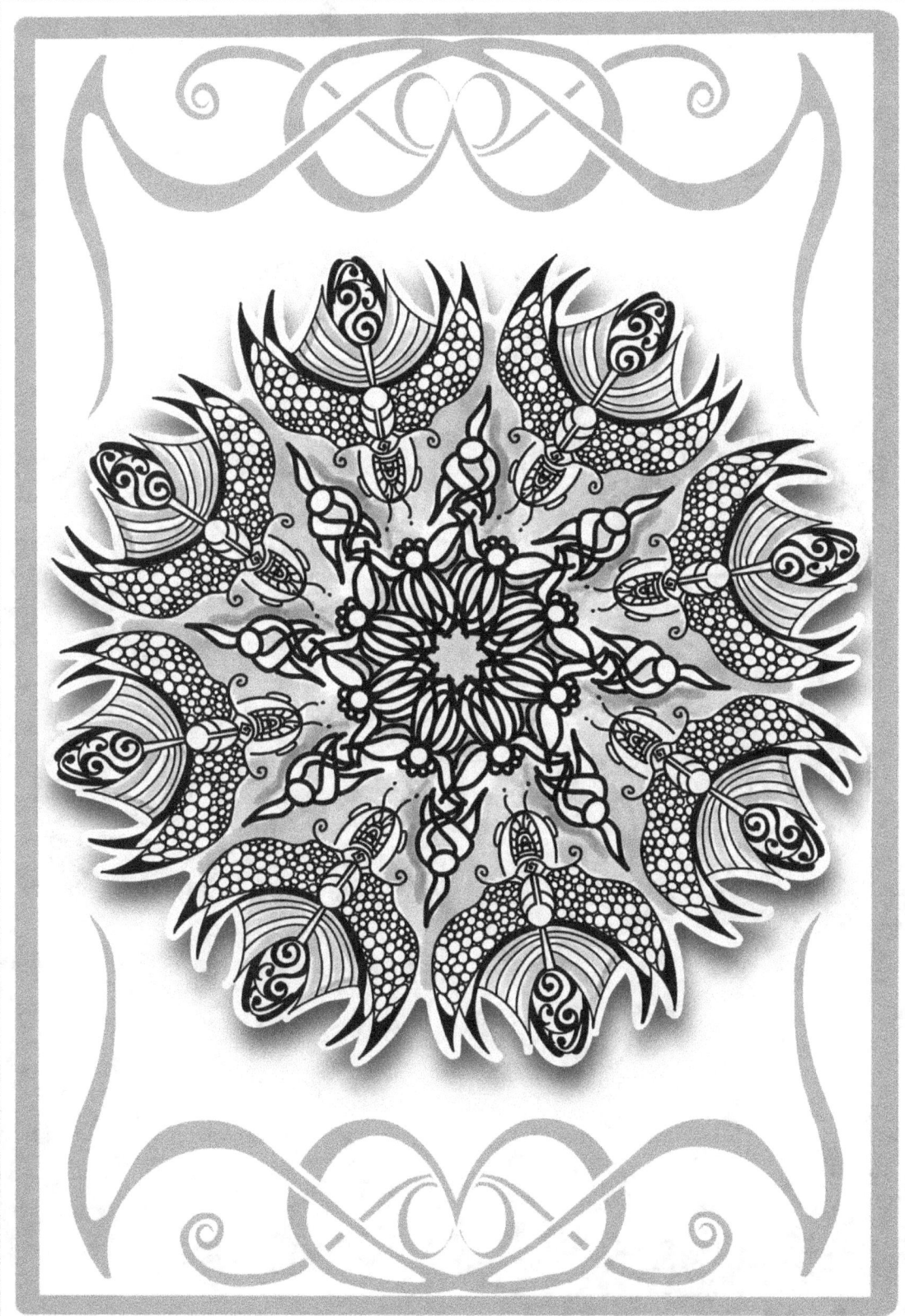

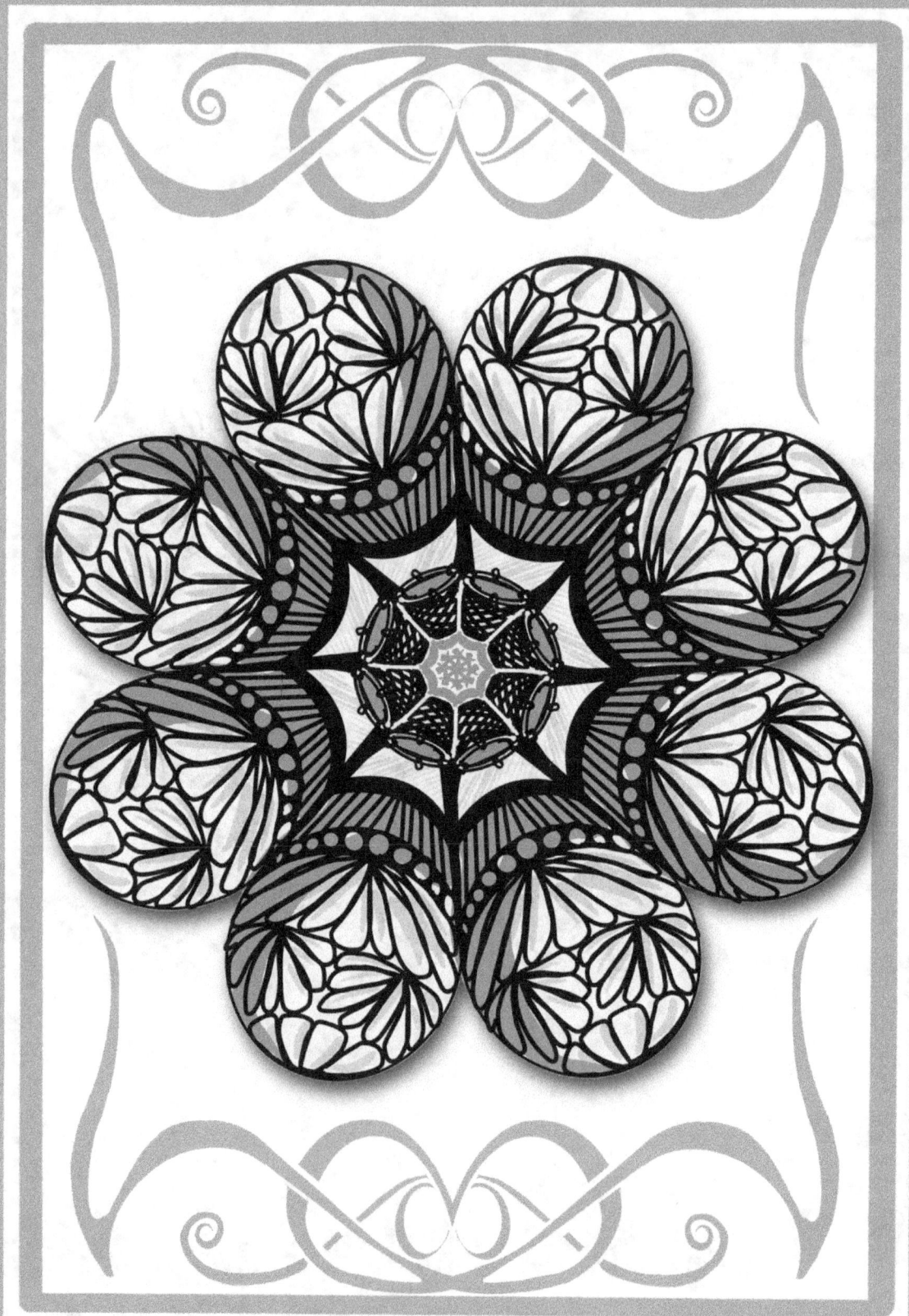

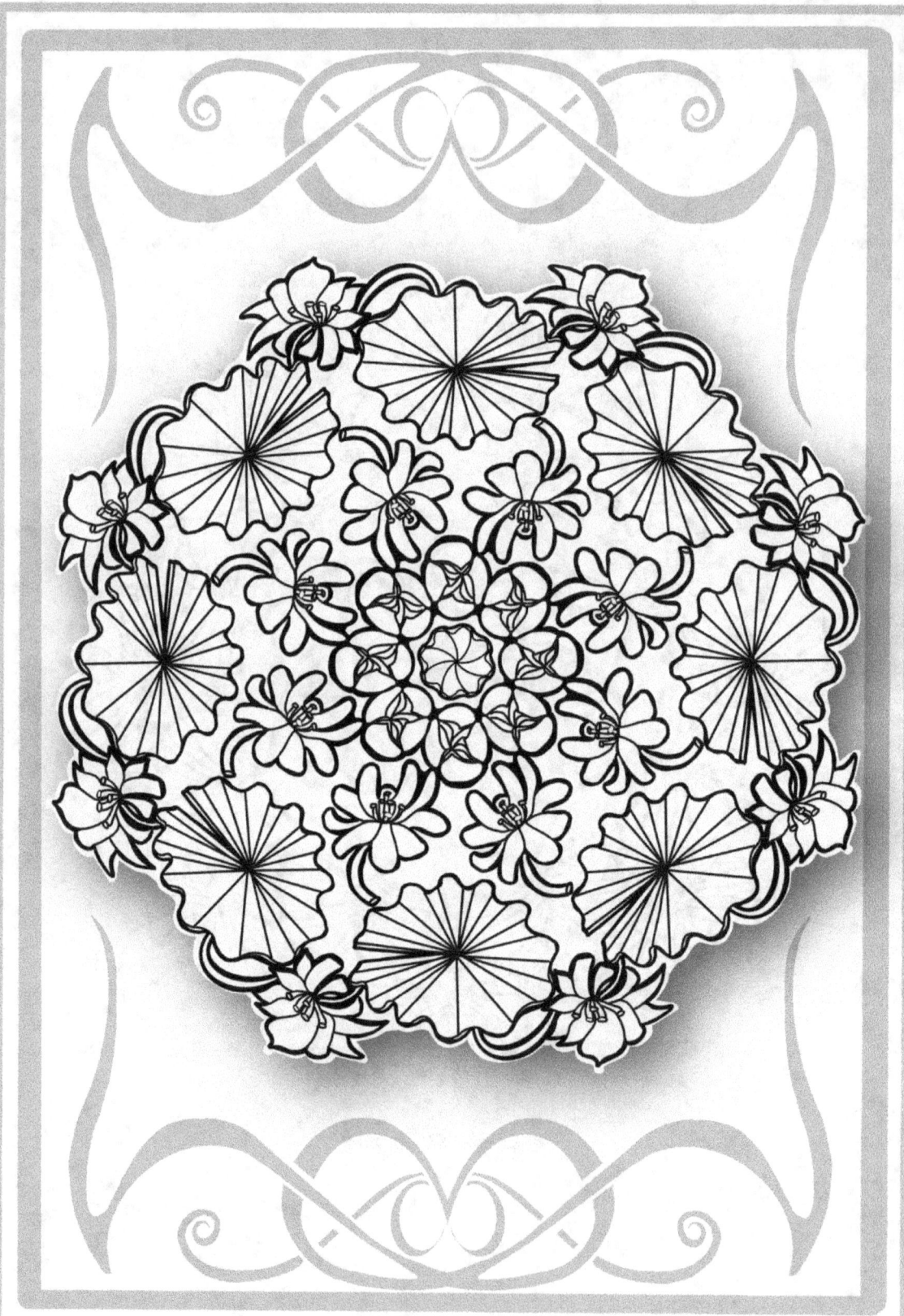